The Wild Here and Now

Susan Charkes

Arboreality Press

ISBN-13:
978-0615902142

ISBN-10:
0615902146

Illustration on p. 4, Edward Hicks, *Peaceable Kingdom*, c. 1834. Courtesy National Gallery of Art, Washington.

CONTENTS

Introduction   4

Here   17

Spring   26

Summer   62

Fall   91

Winter   127

Epilogue   165

Notes   169

Introduction

Out of Africa they came, out of the treeless savannas, westward across the blue ocean, bobbing on swelling waves, trade winds at their back; then up the wide bay, carried on the tide, up the broad river to the rocky shallows, over the steep banks into the dark woods, where they waited in the shadows – waiting to be noticed, and when they were, to lope out into the clearing by the river, to sit and stare, tails flicking, manes glinting in the sun, to sit and wait while a Quaker minister painted them by the river.

He painted them over and over, painted each lion beside a lamb, painted a leopard with kids, cow rubbing noses with bear, a child hovering aloft, pointing the way.

And as he painted them, over and over, the river narrowed to a rocky creek, trees shrank and a bridge rose, and eventually a group of people appeared in the distance. Some, bewigged, wore broadcloth and tricorn hats; others, browner and lightly clad, sported feather headdresses. The central hatted figure spread his arms wide in a gesture of inclusion. All of them focused their attention on a scroll. The frame of the painting the artist adorned with his version of the words of Isaiah, "The lion with the fatling on did move/A little child was leading them in love," and with words of his own: "When the great PENN his famous treaty made/ With Indian chiefs beneath the elm tree's shade."

From his studio in Bucks County, Pennsylvania, Edward Hicks looked out at the landscape of rolling hills, of woods and meandering streams, of farms and villages, and he saw lions. He looked past the lions and he saw the Proprietor, a century and a half past, and he heard the Proprietor saying to Tamanend the Lenape chief, "We meet on the broad pathway of good faith and good-will; no advantage shall be taken on either side, but all shall be openness and love. We are the same as if one man's body was to be divided into two parts; we are of one flesh and one blood." He heard Tamanend reply, "We will live in love with William Penn and his children as long as the creeks and rivers run, and while the sun, moon, and stars endure."

Lions lived here. Here along the Delaware River, north of Philadelphia – Penn's City of Brotherly Love.

Penn lived here, too. Indeed, he named this place for his home county in England, Buckinghamshire, and he built his estate on a point overlooking the broad river, just below the Fall Line: the boulders that mark the meeting place where the redrock hills of the Piedmont subtend the sand and gravel beds of the Atlantic Coastal Plain, where the tide ceases its pushing against the river flowing down to the sea.

Did he know? Did Penn the Peacemaker, visionary of the "Holy Experiment" wherein diverse peoples would accord one another mutual respect − did he intuit that he had sited his home at a place where difference resolves itself into tolerance, each for the other? Mountains meet shore, sea meets river. Lions meet lambs and the people of Europe meet the people of America.

Bucks County is in a fundamental sense today just what it was when the lions roamed: a place of meeting. Its landscape invites encounters by not imposing conditions that demand ways of being. It is neither wilderness nor city, mountain nor plain. It enjoys a four-season climate with extremes tempered by the Gulf Stream. It possesses a not-this, not-thatness, comprising a mosaic of farms and subdivisions, eyeblink villages and brick-and-concrete boroughs, hollow-hidden roadhouses and musclebound malls, old stone crossroads taverns and fast food strips; covered bridges and highway overpasses; steep hemlock-feathered ravines and flat grass-carpeted ballfields; freeform creeks and oval retention ponds; tiny stone Quaker meeting houses and steepled churches. Here, in Penn's home county, where both the Society of Friends and the later-settling German Mennonites call their houses of worship "meeting houses," there are in fact a myriad of meetings: the landscape creates opportunities to encounter the other, to take measure of that which makes us at once us and not them, you and not I.

Laid out as a tipped rectangle, with one long side and one short side along the Delaware (whose great bend at the Fall Line forms one corner), the county gradually increases in elevation and unevenness of terrain west and north from the riverbanks. Its other two sides are essentially cartographic. The 40-mile-long southern bound extends the natural serpentine of the Poquessing creek into a straight-edge. The 20 miles of its western border parallel a line of forested volcanic ridges to the southeast. These rocky, talus-littered diabase hills, from 700 to 900 feet in elevation, are part of a continuous forest extending more than 60 miles, from upper Montgomery County to the west, and east to the Sourland Mountains of New Jersey. The ridges are merely the exposed portions of folded, intruded underground sheets of lithified ancient lava.

Under all that dense, hard volcanic rock is clay. And between the clay and the rock is water, which has no place better to go. Hence, hundreds of acres in western (or "upper") Bucks has been known, since Penn's time, as the Great Swamp. South and east of the swamp is a sparsely settled landscape of gnarly hollows, ragged red cliffs, and tucked-away horse farms. Here, as well, is the county's largest swath of undeveloped land, combining state and county parks and state game lands: forests encircle the 5300-acre Lake Nockamixon, which was created for flood control in1965 by damming the Tohickon Creek. Near the western corner of the county is the sprawling borough of Quakertown – despite its name, a historically German and Mennonite area – a residential/commercial/industrial mélange where big-box stores and new subdivisions bump up against family farms, and where the products of those farms are processed: a century ago tobacco became cigars; today, pork, poultry and milk become ham, sausages and cheese.

The upper county's industrial heritage began long before, in Durham, at the river corner. It was 1727 when iron ore from the hills was first burned there with charcoal from the forests, and the iron sent downriver in flat-bottomed rowboats. Although the ironworks closed 50 years later, those Durham boats earned lasting fame as ferries for George Washington's crossing of the Delaware. The Durham Furnace reopened in the mid eighteenth century, and lasted in that incarnation over 60 years, during which much of the pig iron was sent down to the ports and factories in Philadelphia on mule-drawn barges via the Delaware Canal, a 60-mile channel completed in 1832 that parallels the river from Easton in Northampton County (where the Lehigh River joins the Delaware) to Bristol. Today the canal and its towpath are a state park, providing a nearly unbroken bankside view of the ceaselessly flowing river.

Up to the Fall Line, the Delaware is tidal, broad and deep; upstream it is swifter, shallower and rockier. As a result, navigation – and consequently heavy industry – stopped at the Fall Line, leaving the county's long river side largely undeveloped, except for bank-hugging river towns. The largest of these is New Hope, associated since the late nineteenth century with Pennsylvania Impressionism. The well-funded Michener Art Museum, in Doylestown, showcases the most prominent examples of this still-thriving school of landscape painting. Dis-integrating the light of the river and the shadows of hills and valleys into shards, blurs,

Introduction

smears and points that depict the landscape without
defining it, these works are neither realist nor abstract.
They epitomize the county's in-between quality – even as
they evoke an archaic bucolic heritage, for no school has
yet arisen to paint into beauty the area's glistening traffic
lights, rivers of cars, and mountains of houses.

    From the highlands of the county's upper part flow
the waters of its main creeks – Unami, Perkiomen, Cook,
Tinicum, Tohickon, Deep Run, Neshaminy, Poquessing
(Lenape names almost all of them); and the myriad smaller
creeks and runs, all of which are tributaries or sub-
tributaries of the Delaware. For eons all that water has
carried sediment down from the highlands: silt and clay
from eroding ridges, and nutrient-rich organic matter from
the swamps. Thus favored by alluvial soils, eastern
("lower") Bucks once boasted the most productive farmland
in the state. The riches now lie buried under thousands of
back yards, under landfills and factories, highways, malls
and an amusement park.
    Between the rocky highlands and the riverine
lowlands is central Bucks, a classic Piedmont terrain of
rolling hills of red and gray shale and sandstone. Second-
growth woods of oak, hickory, beech, maple and ash
brindle the hillsides. At the bottom of every one of those
hills is a redrock-bottom creek, meandering through a
shallow valley. Scattered here and there in the valleys are
plowed fields, the rich brown earth studded with red and
gray stones, bordered by walls of stone plucked from those
fields, overseen by a house and a barn built of the same
fieldstones, as if grown from the fields themselves.
Hundred-acre family dairy farms, with their pastures, silos,

stone barns and fields of corn and hay, defined the
landscape as recently as the 1980s. Nowadays the fieldstone
walls and farmhouses and barns are hard to spot in their
new settings: clumps of vinyl-sided brick-faced subdivision
houses, neatly manicured lawns and mulched beds of
perennials. Small farms – many preserved by local
government or conservancies – still form part of the fabric
of the landscape, but nowadays they are embroidery, no
longer the warp and woof of a living rural culture.

Bucks County's 622 square miles were thinly settled,
its populace mainly farmers and merchants, for the first 250
years after Penn's 1682 arrival. Settlement followed the
river and the larger creeks, since those provided both
transportation and the power for mills that formed most of
the early commercial centers. Early main roads, used
primarily by farmers to get their crops to market, were laid
over Indian trading routes. The first federal census in 1790
counted only about 25,000 residents; at the end of the 19th
century the county's population had not even tripled. Even
as late as the 1930s, as Terry McNealy notes in his
magnificent *Bucks County: an Illustrated History*, Bucks led the
state in vegetable production; the value of its crop was
exceeded nationwide only by a few counties in California
and Florida. In 1945, two-thirds of the county was still
farmland.

In the decade following the Second World War the
county was profoundly altered. First came the introduction
of high-density residential development, with the building
of Levittown (18,000-plus homes for more than 50,000
people sprawling over four municipalities), and the
introduction of heavy industry, with the construction of

U.S. Steel's Fairless works – both in lower Bucks. Next came the improvement and expansion of several interstate highways that traversed the county's eastern and southern borders. Now development raced along roadways rather than accumulating along waterways. Farms and woods were left only along the disappearing byways. Between 1940 and 1960 the county's population grew threefold, then doubled again over the next 40 years. In 2010 over 625,000 people called Bucks County home; farmland occupied less than a fifth of its 387,000 land acres.

Yet Bucks County is also home to over 2000 species of plants (the most diverse collection of any county in the state) and more than 200 bird species. Deer and turkey are abundant not only in forested state game lands but also in suburban backyards. Shad still churn their way up the Delaware to spawn in spring. The Quakertown Swamp is home to eastern Pennsylvania's largest great blue heron colony. Over 50,000 acres, more than 13,000 of them farmland, have been preserved as open space through state, local and private conservation efforts.

This above all is Penn's heritage. It is the countryside. A countryside on steroids, perhaps: one that is noisier, dirtier, denser and (at night) brighter than the countryside that Penn knew. But still, in its essence, it is country: a landscape in which human impact is neither total nor absent. A landscape in which humans share the wealth of water, soil, green leaves, air and light with their fellow beings, sentient and otherwise.

Though he founded one, Penn had no great love for cities. "The Country Life is to be Preferred," he wrote, for there we see the Works of God; but in Cities little else but the Works of Men: And the one makes a better Subject for our Contemplation than the other. As Puppets are to Men, and Babies to Children, so is Man's Workmanship to God's: We are the Picture, he the Reality. God's Works declare his Power, Wisdom and Goodness; but Man's Works, for the most part, his Pride, Folly and Excess. The one is for use, the other, chiefly, for Ostentation and Lust. The Country is both the Philosopher's Garden and his Library, in which he Reads and Contemplates the Power, Wisdom and Goodness of God. It is his Food as well as Study; and gives him Life, as well as Learning…A Sweet and Natural Retreat from Noise and Talk, and allows opportunity for Reflection, and gives the best Subjects for it. In short, 't is an Original, and the Knowledge and Improvement of it, Man's oldest Business and Trade, and the best he can be of.

Knowledge *and* Improvement? The inherent contradiction between the value of Contemplating the Works of God while also Improving upon these Works of Power, Wisdom and Goodness is at the heart of the landscape of the country, and what is now the suburbs. It is that same not-this not-that-ness, a bothness, trying to have it both ways. Neither city nor wilderness, but a *better* wilderness. One we can live with. From the time of the Lenape to the present day, Bucks County has seen waves of settlers come to its human-scale, comfortable landscape, contemplate its temperate air, its rich woods, its picturesque valleys and sparkling streams, and then decide that the best thing to do here is to *improve* it. Clear the woods, dam the streams, plant crops, build houses and lay out roads: in general make it easier and safer to stay here and get from here to there.

Long before William Levitt and Toll Brothers, William Penn was the Delaware Valley's first major land developer: the first to realize that its value could be translated into cash and communities. In his 1683 "Letter to the Free Society of Traders," a promotional brochure for his new colony, Penn described the air, water, soil, seasons, produce (natural and artificial), living creatures, plants and flowers. In these attributes, "the country," he noted – with characteristic Quaker understatement – "is not to be despised."

Penn described various native fruits in great detail: mulberry, chestnut, walnut, plums, strawberries, cranberries, blackberries, huckleberries and "grapes of divers sorts." As to these last, Penn mused:

> It is disputable with me, whether it be best to fall to refining the fruits of the country, especially the grape, by the acre and skill of art, or send for foreign stems and sets, already good and approved. It seems most reasonable to believe, that a thing grows best where it naturally grows, but will hardly be equaled by another species of the same kind that does not naturally grow there. But to solve the doubt, I intend …to try both and hope the consequences will be as good wine as any European countries of the same latitude do yield.

Here it is: the having it both ways – the wild native and the improved import.

As with fruits, so with people.

Pennsylvania was founded on the rock of utopianism. Penn envisioned a society that would be "an example..,to the nations." A "Holy Experiment," he called it. Not merely a refuge for his fellow persecuted Quakers, it would be a place whose inhabitants practiced the spiritual principles that others merely professed. "Love, forgive, help and serve one another, and let the people learn by your example, as well as by your power, the happy life of concord," he instructed his colonists. Its 1682 Frame of Government enacted the ideal of diverse people each of whom respected the right of the others to be who they were – albeit within limits. "All persons living in this province who confess and acknowledge the one almighty and eternal God to be the creator, upholder and ruler of the world, and that hold themselves obliged in conscience to live peaceably and justly in civil society, shall in no ways be molested or prejudiced for their religious persuasion or practice...."

Because Penn himself judged the native Lenape people's spiritual practice to be monotheism, all could live, in "openness and love," under the shade of the peace tree. The wild native as well as the domesticated import.

Hicks made visible the connection between a peaceable kingdom where humans live in loving harmony with wild animals, all giving up their natural enmity, and a treaty of loving brotherhood between peoples who naturally fear each other. What forges the connection is a loving bond of acceptance – not the erasure of difference but the neutralization of it.

But is diversity a matter of toleration? or celebration? Is it merely acceptance of the wild? or is it the seeking out of the wild? the joy of going forth and meeting it?

Through wildness comes peace. The peace of love, a force grounded on acceptance but growing out of it to celebration. We will never see the lions unless we go and look for them. And they will only come out when we are ready to paint them into existence – when we are ready to celebrate their wild nature, and ours too. So is our spirit exalted.

By the time Hicks painted his Peaceable Kingdoms, the peace had been shattered and the Kingdom scattered. Penn made his "famous treaty" on the Delaware in 1682. Not a treaty declaring the end of hostilities – for hostilities there were none – it was a "treaty of brotherhood" between peoples. A mere 50 years later, the infamous Walking Purchase had effectively abrogated it. In 1732 several of Penn's descendants "discovered" a 1686 deed by which the Lenape supposedly sold a tract of land extending from Wrightstown, at the (then) northern bound of the county, through the wilderness, as far as a man could walk in a day and a half; at a typical speed this might be 40 miles. Beyond the questionable provenance of this deed, its effect was compounded by one of the more disgraceful episodes of Pennsylvania history. The Penns cleared a trail through the thick woods and engaged the three fastest walkers in the colony. In 1737, the fleetest of them "walked" 65 miles in 18 hours. Then, from the endpoint the surveyors drew a boundary extending northeast, rather than due east to the river as tradition dictated, embracing 1200 square miles, essentially the entire "mouth" of Pennsylvania's eastern border.

Perfidy had replaced peaceful coexistence as the ruling principle between the two peoples; love beat a retreat. The Lenape began to move west, into Pennsylvania's Wyoming Valley, and they kept going. The Treaty Elm – the tree said to be the one that shaded the peacemakers – stood until 1810, when it came down in a storm. Scions of the elm were planted all over. There is one on an Oklahoma reservation – where the Lenape now live.

This time, Improvement had run the wild native out.

Yet creeks and rivers still run, and the sun, moon and stars look down on them.

And lions lurk in the shadows of the woods. They are waiting – waiting for us to see them. Waiting for us to *want* to see them, to heal the shattered peace. To seek them out at a place of meeting. And then to celebrate our being in this place together. To live in love.

HERE

What would the world be, once bereft
Of wet and of wildness? Let them be left,
O let them be left, wildness and wet;
Long live the weeds and the wilderness yet.
Gerard Manley Hopkins, "Inversnaid"

I crouched as low as possible to avoid scraping my face on the branches of a hickory tree whose roots were some twenty feet below. I was balanced on top of a fencerow of treadless tires stacked three high in alternating courses. The tires were nearly invisible, overgrown with thickets of honeysuckle, raspberry and multiflora rose. Behind me was the rear yard of an auto repair shop, littered with rusting engines, dented hubcaps, chipped fenders and miscellaneous parts. A divided highway wrapped around the shop's main building. The tire fence stretched for hundreds of feet in both directions: one end disappeared into the highway embankment; the other, into a hedgerow of shrubs lining a drainage ditch. Upslope from the ditch were the back lots of new-car dealers, where row upon row of unblemished vehicles stood waiting their turn to be called to the showroom, a car-lifetime away from their inevitable end in the parts pile at the rear of the repair shop.

The back lots of the car shops, new and old, formed two sides of a rough triangle. The hypotenuse was drawn by a creek. Between the creek and the back lots there was a woods: a canopy of hickories, oaks and ashes towering over clumps of spicebush, witch hazel, arrowwood and

17

dogwood; the floor a dark mat of leaves, twigs and branches interlaced with a network of streams and ditches that wound down to the creek. The woods hugged the base of a twenty-foot cliff of backfill that was topped, behind the repair-shop leg of the triangle, by the tire fence. As I balanced on top of the fence, peering through the tangle of tree branches, I could see a patch of light green down below. Light green meant new leaves. Spring had just arrived; the flat white winter light had started to soften. The air was still cold and dry, a strong wind flung highway grit into in my eyes. Cars whipped past, accelerating around the bend, a constant stream that emitted a low drone with a Doppler pulse.

High above the drone, I heard a short chirping "peep." Then another. Then silence, then some more peeps, and more, and soon a chorus of peeps peeping their peepingest to keep up, bursting out of the pond like a sonic waterspout, raining sound down in torrents, then less peepfully slowing their peeping, but a quick hard slowing like stepping on the brakes, slowing until there were no more peeps. When it was over, for a long moment peeping seemed to reverberate and fill the air, a silence drowning out the highway drone. As if my ears, once accustomed to the all-encompassing peeping chorus, would respond to nothing else. For an instant the world belonged to the choristers. They had made of it a wall of sound that kept out everything else that didn't matter to them at that moment in that place.

Weeds, wet and wildness were in that place.

It is, perhaps, an affront to Gerard Manley Hopkins to invoke his blessing, as it were, on this spot. After all, the poem whose closing stanza is this essay's epigraph took as its subject a dramatic waterfall near Loch Lomond in the

Here

Scottish Highlands: a tumbling, roaring, frothing natural wonder in the heart of the most storied landscape in the British Isles, Rob Roy's own countryside.

There were no bagpipes here, in this hidden woodland pond, only a chorus of spring peepers: thumbnail-size frogs with Valkyrie-sized voices. This bit of froggy woods is the kind of marginal place that gets overlooked in our functionalist culture. Too wet to build on, to mow, to cultivate, or to clear for timber. Tucked between places devoted to the machines that both define the way we live now and literally shape our world.

The world that inhabits the essays in this book lies in Bucks County, Pennsylvania, about 25 miles northwest of Philadelphia. The landscape, along the eastern fringe of the Piedmont lowlands between the Delaware River and the Appalachian mountains, is like a wimpled crazy-quilt: long ridgefolds of red shale hills webbed with streams and mottled with woods. Once part of a vast continuous forest – the "Penn's Woods" for which the state was named – the area became, within three centuries after European settlement, a rural patchwork of small family farms: neat rectangular cultivated fields separated by stone walls, hedgerows, woodlots and marshes. Nowadays, 50 years of suburbanization have virtually tilled the farms under. Some endure, but most have been turned into residential subdivisions, neat squares of mowed turfgrass separated by trimmed hedges and sealed driveways.

In this tamed world, the wild persists. Despite centuries of human intervention here, creeks course down rocky russet hillsides like gravy on mounds of mashed red potatoes; fields and woods speckle the landscape like salt and pepper. The bear, elk, and wolf, who shared the pre-colonial forested hills with the indigenous Lenape, are long gone; so are less-romantic species like the bog turtle, the upland sandpiper, and the regal fritillary. But between the roads, the houses, and the parking lots, the playfields and shopping centers, in amongst the shaved lawns and the mulched nature strips – in a landscape of leftovers – the wild persists.

Outside my home-office window, beginning about late March, the spring peepers start to sing in the evenings. Just when the days start to retain their warmth past twilight; when Ursa the Bear begins to best Orion the Hunter in their annual contest for pride of place in the night sky; when rain-sodden mire devours the boots of the walker; when the ground-hugging ephemeral wildflowers tilt their faces up to the bees tumbling out of their hives, and tree buds doff the nightcaps that have kept their heads warm through winter – then the frogs begin to call.

They call from a pond a quarter-mile off, hidden somewhere in the woods beyond the fallow field secreted behind the backyards of the houses across the street. These peepers have been calling every spring for as long as I've lived here. In drought years and flood years, they've kept calling. The noise from the nearby main road has gotten louder. New houses have been built around the edges of the field. The woodcock, the red-winged blackbird, and the field sparrow no longer sing from the field; their former homes are now three-story foyers. Still the frogs call. Their chorus pierces the din of civilization, a blast like an airhorn from a truck barreling toward you on a mountain curve. Or like a shofar, blown from the top of the mountain.

As humans relentlessly increase their control over the landscape, there are fewer and fewer places where wild things can flourish. They are squeezed out and hemmed in, starved and run over, extirpated deliberately and accidentally.

What does it mean to be wild, in a world pervaded with human influence?

What would it mean to be human, in a world bereft of the wild?

"In Wildness is the preservation of the world," Thoreau famously wrote. Or not so famously: he is just as often misquoted as having said instead, "In Wilderness is the preservation of the world."

The distinction makes a difference, for wilderness is, by definition, a place untrammeled by man. Few of us live in, or even near, a wilderness. Wilderness conjures up vast spaces, hard-to-get to places, rare animals, extreme conditions. The Alaskan tundra, the interior Rocky Mountains, the Sonoran desert.

Wildness, though, is all around, wherever you are. The wild is what humans didn't create, didn't tame or domesticate. Wildness may live with you, but it is not yours.

In his essay "Walking," the source of the "Wildness" line, Thoreau extolled the benefits of walking – but not just walking, walking in nature. "When we walk we naturally go to the fields and woods; what would become of us if we walked only in a garden or a mall?"

Thoreau walked, not in a remote wilderness, but in the countryside around Concord, Massachusetts, a prosperous, sophisticated New England town. A ten-mile radius of his house, or an afternoon's walk, was sufficient to provide an "absolutely new prospect" every time he ventured outside.

The prospects have narrowed for most of us since Thoreau's time. The countryside around Concord was either farmed or left alone. And a man could walk for hours without seeing another person, nor even a house. There are still places like this in America, though few of us live there. Our landscapes are atomized into disjoint pieces, we are confined on all sides by the built environment. For many of us, we have to take a car to get to a place that looks anything like Thoreau's Concord country. Indeed, his prediction has come to pass: "At present, in this vicinity, the best part of the land is not private property; the landscape is not owned, and the walker enjoys comparative freedom. But possibly the day will come when it will be partitioned off into so-called pleasure grounds, in which a few will take a narrow and exclusive pleasure only, – when fences shall be multiplied, and man traps and other engines invented to confine men to the public road; and walking over the surface of God's earth, shall be construed to mean trespassing on some gentleman's grounds."

Like the woods I can't get to, behind someone's house. Where the peepers sing.

Or like the place behind the auto repair shop.

Peepers will call as often from puddles and roadside ditches as they do from woodland ponds. They don't need a permanent body of water; a vernal pool, which forms in springtime and dries up in summer, is sufficient. Their requirements are simple, but logical. The males sing from plants in or around the water, filling a vocal sac almost as big as the rest of their body with air and expelling it forcefully, up to 4000 times an hour. Neighboring males sing alternately, and the net effect is a chorus. An interested female peeper will swim up to a male and release a clutch of 800-1000 eggs, which the male fertilizes in the water. The eggs drift away, typically becoming attached singly or in groups of two or three to an underwater stem. The young hatch within 6-12 days. These tadpoles metamorphose into juvenile frogs over the next three months; tailed froglets can climb out of the water within six weeks to complete their transformation on land (a helpful adaptation if you're likely to be born in a temporary pond). By midsummer, the frogs have dispersed back into the woods where they live in the leaf litter and lower reaches of shrubs and other plants, eating spiders, ants, beetles and other small woodland creatures. In the fall, they burrow beneath the soil to hibernate, frozen solid, until they are revived by the vernal sun.

So to make a wild home, peepers need, first of all, the sun. They need the warmth of the spring sun to enable water to flow, so that they can come out of hibernation and breed. Thus peepers need, also, water. And weeds: leafy plants to sing from, and to hide from predators under, and to attach eggs to. They need woods, too, because they find food and cover from predators there. And they need spiders, insects, and other small woodland creatures because that's what they eat. And earth, because that's where the woods grows, not in cement planters placed strategically around a parking lot. And air, because without air to pass sound waves the peep of a peeper would die before it left the vocal sac.

Sun, Earth, water, leafy plants, woods, little woodland creatures, air.

They don't need me.

It's sort of comforting to know that. Here's this world we're born into that has been going on since a long long time before we got here, and it goes on without our having to think about it. Day after day, year after year. Millennium after millennium. Sun needs no memo to make it shine; Earth no loan to orbit; water no contract to flow, frogs no thought of ours to sing. It's a relief to know that the weight of the world isn't on our shoulders. It's one less thing to worry about. There's a freedom, a lightness in that realization.

I need them.

I need the hold they have on me, the way they tug me out of myself, into the web of dependency and consequence that connects life on Earth, the anticipation of the coming season and the memory of past ones. I need what they have that I don't have, to remind me that I am not sufficient, and I need what they need – earth, air, sun and water – to remind me that I am one with them.

They need us. They need us to care about them, and about the places we share, and about the places we can't share because to share would be to destroy. They need us to trek into the forgotten place that somebody else owns, behind the tire fence next to the highway, to stand on the edge, balanced between the wild and the tame, and face the wild. They need us to look out the window, or better, to open the window, or even better, to go outside, to listen for the calls borne on the spring wind that know no human-imposed boundaries. They need us to pay attention, and by so doing, to honor their presence.

Wild is what we have in common: a place to live a life, and time in which to live it.

To know the wild, look from where you are, listen from where you stand. Here and now.

Now

Spring

Dawnsong and Sundance

They sleep, some with clenched toes grasping a high branch; some tucked into a nook at the base of a shrub; others hunkered in a portholed tree cavity. No matter where, she finds them. She reaches out, touches them ever so lightly, brushes their wings with the tips of her rosy fingers. They blink awake.

Eos opens the gates; the curtain rises on the cusp of morning.

Now they sing. Robin: merrily, verily, see! He has the stage to himself at first, soloing in the hinterlands of light, over and over. Now Cardinal whistles: hear, hear, cheep cheep cheep cheep cheep cheep. Finches buzz-slide up and down the scale, each vying to outwarble the other. Song sparrow scats bipbip bopbop ooopooplyoopdop. Carolina wren must have the last and loudest word: keytettle keytettle, tea! All together now!

Out in the country, few sounds compete with the dawn chorus; nor are there leaves on early-spring trees to muffle song. Even the tiniest of voices finds a place in the choir, and the woods resound with reverberations.

In-town birds, though, must out-sing not just each other but the growling garbage truck, the beeping backhoe, the screaming siren, the piped-out music from the smoothie store. They've evolved to be loudmouths. The sweet, the soft and the sultry don't make enough noise in spring to attract a mate; only the belters, the avian Ethel Mermans and Michael Boltons, survive.

One morning each week, Doylestown's streets are quiet. Birds vocalize into the void vacated by commerce, accompanying the chiming churchbells, praising the glory of the dawn. It is, after all, the Sun's day.

The chorus builds in volume. Helios arrives, his chariot ablaze. Flames of pink, red, now yellow, white. He passes and is gone. Light fills the sky.

Now the chorus stops. It's time to go to work. Time to eat, time to court, time to gather moss.

In the fullness of light, the a cappella dance begins. Sun warms the air, clothing it with substance; warm air curtsies to the ground.

Dew shakes off sleep and opens one eye. Not time yet.

Flowers unbelt their nightrobes to reveal perky pink spring dresses, for sunwarmth brings visitors. The visitors themselves stir in their underground nests, under leaves and rocks, in sawdusty burrows. They rush out, wings abuzz. The air swarms with their newborn glee as they charge about in search of nectar, now this way now that, zong, zang, zongg!

Dew opens its other eye and blinks. Not time yet.

Hiding in shadow, butterflies wait for their cue, wings folded drab side out: gray, tan, brown. Cold wings can't fly. They're earthbound, stuck fast like last winter's moldering leaves.

Warm air tries rocks next. Cold rocks like to be cold. You can't make us warm up, they taunt air. Air sighs, sits. Waits. Rocks are stubborn, but they come around. Little by little, crumb by crumb, crusty old rocks change their tune. They dance, but in a reverie, reflectively. Slow but sure, rocks give back the warmth they've been collecting. A shiver, a shimmy, and air is on its way. Up up up.

Dew stretches, rolls over, sits. Dew puts on its spangly crown and leaps into the air. Dance, dew, dance! up to the sun!

Now, on warm dry rocks, butterflies settle softly and unfold their wings. Come, sun, they plead. Their spreadwing colors are an offering. Orange, blue, purple, copper: your colors, Helios! we praise you! bless us! And blessings multiply. Sunwarmed wings finally flutter. They rise and fall, up and down, updown and downup.

I sit, still and silent, in sunlight. My heart sings; my soul dances.

What's Happening in an "Empty Field"

There's something about an empty field that awakens the urge to put something there. For some it may be a farm, for others, a ballfield, and still others, houses. A meadow, like a blank canvas that calls out to the artist to paint something, seems to hold the potential for creation.

Even Mother Nature is not immune to the desire. Given time, patience and, most important, water, trees will colonize a meadow and transform it into a forest.

But for those who get to know a field, it can never seem empty. Take, for example, the residents of Country Greene, a development constructed in Plumstead Township, Bucks County, in the 1990's. Houses are arranged around the eight acres of Jennifer Schweitzer Park, much of which is left as a "natural" meadow year-round. Initially, neighbors adamantly resisted the idea of an unmowed field. But, according to Nancy Minich of Delaware Valley College, who consulted on the design of the park, once they lived with the field in their backyards, they came to know and love it. Now, you couldn't make them give it up.

What is it about a field? Spend a year with an "empty" field and you'll see that it has value, not just for what it can become, but for what it is.

It's the sequence of colors that gives away the life rhythms within. Winter's dull beige and tan softens gradually with green. Abruptly the green is laid over with a riot of yellow as mustard plants burst into bloom, celebrating the return of the sun. Yellow gives way to white, as daisies, wild carrot and, finally, asters arrive like so many maids of honor, while milkweed pods burst and fling silky tangles of seeds up into the waiting sky. Late summer burnishes the field with yellow again, this time the darker, deeper yellow of goldenrods, whose heads gradually dry on the plumes and fade to brown. Waving in the winter winds, above white snow-covered ground, these noble natives refuse to go gently into that dark night. All winter they stand, battered by wind and weather, their presence recalling summer's warmth. When the first green shoots of spring emerge, the goldenrods bend reluctantly, bowing down to their upstart successors.

Colors move, too. In summertime, yellow, orange, white and blue wings flit up and down and all around, as butterflies do the insect equivalent of a pub crawl from one flowerhead to another. Bluebirds dart back and forth from trees to the field, hunting for insects; goldfinches make quick undulating flights as they gather seeds; a gray kingbird flashes white as it wheels and turns, snatching food from the air. A red fox bursts out of a clump of brush, intent on its prey.

And then there's field music. In spring, courting birds give daily song recitals. In summer, crickets take over the stage. Fall and winter, it is the wind that plays, blowing through standing stems and dangling leaves to create a symphony.

Yet the most important work a field does can't be seen, or heard. It's underground. The field acts likes a giant sponge. When it rains, plants take up some water through their roots, but most of the water filters down slowly through the soil. Eventually it reaches the groundwater aquifer. This "recharge" of the aquifer is crucial to replenishing the supply of water on which all life – including humans – depends.

There's no such thing as an empty field. A field fills your soul, but it never empties itself.

Fly in the Ointment

There are no bugs in Pennsylvania Impressionist landscapes. This is surprising, since the painters of this school prided themselves on doing the actual painting *en plein air* – outdoors, in the elements, where bugs are wont to frolic.

Early one spring morning, before a visit to the collection of these Bucks County artists at the Michener Museum in Doylestown, PA, I happened to have some business that entailed a tramp through a field bordering a tree-lined stream. From every angle, the views could have been framed in a painting. A trace of fog lingered in the air, softening the early morning light. Tender young leaves graced the branches of spicebush, viburnum and red maple.

The woods on both sides of the stream were carpeted with low flowers: splashes of white, pink and yellow. In the field, the sunlight fashioned diamond necklaces out of dew-caught spiderwebs suspended in tufts of grass. A bluebird flashed in constant motion from the field to a tree.

The bluebird was catching insects.

And, of course, so were the spiders, not to mention the flowers.

Blackflies hovered around my head and that of my companion, circling and diving, occasionally landing, and generally making pests of themselves until we gave in and departed for more civilized surroundings. Several flies decided to stake a claim on my person, so for hours afterward I would suddenly feel a tickle, or an itch, and reach around to the back of my neck, or under my shirt, or other odd places, where I would pick off a small winged creature.

The Impressionists must have been plagued by bugs. After all, they worked in an era before the invention of nasty-but-effective insect repellants. I defy anyone to stand in a meadow overlooking the Delaware River in summer, long enough to paint a scene of sun-drenched hills, without attracting a crowd of six-legged admirers.

The absence of bugs from the paintings is telling. What is omitted is small, flighty and annoying. The first two qualities make the bug hard to paint, although the same could also be said of the evanescent qualities of light that these artists evoked to such magical effect. The last quality, though, is the most significant. Bugs are buggy.

Art is all about arrangement, selection and control. Bugs are all about the next meal. Rarely seen in paintings (other than those by bird specialists), insects are literally uncomfortable reminders of things at the limits of human perception. As visual creatures, we are bothered by things we cannot see because we don't know what they are doing. Insects, especially the flying kind, appear and disappear out of thin air. Oh, we love our butterflies and even dragonflies, but they are a nice size and they have a reassuring habit of standing still long enough for our feeble brains to register them.

There is a difference between responding to the harmony, poetry and beauty in the world around us, made evident by the arts, and trying to turn the world into art by selecting, arranging and controlling our environment. Suppose we could remove the bugs from the picture altogether and just leave in the stuff we like. Birds and frogs would starve. Unpollinated flowers would fade away and not return. Detritus would pile up. Eventually we would suffocate under a blanket of dust uneaten by mites.

Spring sunlight streaming into my bedroom window wakes me up with the promise of perfection. Drawn by an irresistible pull into spending hours outdoors, I have in mind a picture of a beautiful spring day and I bound into it – feeling the sun's warmth, enjoying the flowers, listening to the birdsong and trickling streams, measuring the expanse of earth and sky. And every spring I end up with an itchy red welt. I have never seen the bug that bites me. I don't think it is from a bug at all, at least not a specific bug. Just a bite from the universal bug: the one that says, "Life's not all pretty pictures." The one that says, "You're not just an observer in this world. You're part of it. You can flick me off, wave me away, step on me, screen me out, but you can't avoid me. Deny me at your peril. Paint that."

"."

Mind the Gap

What is the distance between here and there?

Here, I am outside, sitting on a chair, at a low plastic table, upon which is a rectangular piece of particle board that serves as a typing support for my electronic organizer. *There*, perched on top of the device just above the screen, is a jumping spider: the size of my pinky-nail, its rear yellow section spotted black, its forward section a fuzzy dark gray.

The spider is distracting me from my task. The distance between me and the spider is an arm's length. I reach out with a pen and gently pick up the spider to move it. It spins out an elastic thread and springs back. We play at this a few times. Finally, I thrust it firmly onto the table; the thread does not hold and the spider stays put.

I look up from my typing a minute later. It is standing on the edge of the board, facing me. From here, it appears to be waving, its enlarged front legs moving constantly.

Using a magnifying lens, I shorten the distance between us by a factor of ten. This close, I can see its main eyes, a pair of black points each no bigger than the dot over the "i" on my screen. Its forward-most legs wave in complicated figure 8's and the front section bounces up and down.

What is the meaning of this message? Between there and here, between the intention and the reception, is a chasm. But what is the nature of the misunderstanding? Has this spider mistaken me for an outsized rendition of its opposite number, greeting me as it would a potential mate? And why not? It is only when we are most open to the unexpected that great insights occur.

Spring

The spider drops partway below the board's edge and faces away from me. Half under the board, half on the side, it surveys the area. A tiny fly lands on the board and meanders around, never getting closer than four or five inches from the edge. The spider watches it. The fly leaves. It returns. It ambles closer this time, a thumb's length. Too close. The spider leaps. The distance between the two of them is zero. Fly in mouth, the spider jumps backwards to its starting place. The entire action takes place in a fraction of a second. This is how an instant must be defined.

The fly disappears slowly into the spider's maw. This is another chasm between us. I do not willingly ingest these flies, although I cannot always avoid doing so while speeding downhill on a bicycle. But the distance between the spider and the fly is always zero. They are predator and prey; their relationship is well-established, and the message, the one conveyed by the jump of the jumping spider, cannot be misunderstood.

Its meal over, the spider turns toward me and commences waving again. Really, this is too distracting. With a stick, I move the spider to the ground and return to my work at the keyboard. Minutes later, I look up to see it again, waving.

Enough. I cannot bear the responsibility of failing to answer. I walk away, putting space between us.

What is the distance between here and there? No greater than the distance between my lowering foot and the ground, as an ant scurries underneath. There is time to avert the collision. If there is time, one is obligated to do so. There may be an urgent message to be delivered.

Rabbit, Rabbit

On the first day of the month, make sure the first words you say are "rabbit, rabbit." This will bring you a month's worth of good luck. Unless, that is, you believe in the variation that requires you to say "rabbit, rabbit, rabbit," or the one that has you saying "white rabbit" in order to earn the same rewards.

Early on the first day of May, I was standing in the yard, enjoying a moment before leaving for work. Mornings are not my specialty, so it is a challenge to remember to say "rabbit rabbit" rather than "who left this on the stairs" first thing before coffee, but this time around I had, and already some of that promised luck appeared to be operating. The sun was shining; the air was cool and sweet and clear. Pale green light filtered through young tree leaves. Then I glanced down and saw the rabbit.

The Eastern cottontail is a common resident of suburban yards and rural areas. Its favored foods include not only vegetables grown in gardens and fodder grasses planted in farm fields, but also the leaves of lawn weeds such as dandelions and plantains. Add shrubs for cover (foundation plantings or hedgerows), and you have perfect rabbit habitat.

The rabbit was just a few feet away from me. Our eyes locked, but neither of us made a move. I decided to give the rabbit a chance to escape into the undergrowth, so I looked in the other direction. I gave it a good five seconds, then looked back. The rabbit had not budged. "OK, have it your way," I said. "It's a beautiful morning, isn't it?" The rabbit was silent, unfazed by my attempt at conversation. I took the hint. We stood there, we two, together, in silence, not moving.

Now, it was quite likely that the rabbit was not moving because it hoped I would not notice it. This is a typical cottontail defense tactic. On the other hand, maybe, just maybe, it too was enjoying the moment. In either case, I felt that a small dome of peace had descended on the two of us, briefly. There we were, each of us at home in the world. For a few minutes I had the same experience of the elements as did the rabbit; the green light and the sunshine and the clean cool air all felt the same way to me as they did to the rabbit. And we were experiencing them together.

After a few minutes, the sun was still shining but the clock was ticking. "Well, gotta go," I noted amiably. I sauntered away, then looked back: the rabbit was gone. Off to find breakfast.

Rabbits in the yard have acquired a reputation as pests, but then again, few large creatures have escaped such disapprobation from modern humans. Groundhogs, squirrels, geese, deer, foxes, coyotes, wild turkeys and even bear all compete with us for space, and eat the stuff that is on "our" property. The litany of complaints about our fellow beings is long. Crows are noisy, vultures ugly, toads warty; ticks spread disease, mosquitoes bite, bees sting; mice eat grain, ants eat crumbs, slugs eat leaves, voles eat roots, moles make hills, skunks stink, raccoons get into garbage, bats get in your hair, spiders are dirty, snakes are scary. Some of these are true, some false, some a matter of opinion.

In an earlier phase of my life, I was involved in municipal bond financing. Bond issuers would obtain insurance to get better debt ratings. The standard used by the rating agencies when reviewing these insurance policies was that "all risks are covered." Not that there are no risks, mind you, only that they are covered. Someone will make up for the loss.

Luck is just the converse of risk. Risk can be quantified; that's why insurance companies stay solvent. Luck is what can't be quantified. But it sure makes up for the loss. I'll take the risk of being stung, bitten, dirty, scared, or offended; of losing plants and time and money. Give me five minutes with a rabbit in the cool sunshine of the first day of May. Now that's luck.

All risks are covered.

Time to Go A-Maying Again

May. The air is thick with sudden light, as flowers burst into being – painting white, yellow, blue, pink onto the blank canvas of sky and ground. Wind scatters petals like memories of snow; trees fairly drip with fragrance. May comes: we must go.

Who will go a-Maying with me? *A-what?*

> "Who will go a-maying?
>   A-maying – a-maying?
> Over field and fence and through
>   the alders growing dense
> Beside the brook."

In 1912, when Edna St Vincent Millay first read this poem, her audience knew what Maying was:

Spring

> "Come we'll go to a place I know
>> Where every year pink mayflowers grow.
> And home at night come journeying
>> With our arms and hearts
>>> Brim full of spring."

Who knows now?

Maying used to be an American rite of spring. Around May 1, people would journey to woods and meadows to gather spring wildflowers, carrying home armfuls of blossoms. They might wear flowers in their hair, or decorate their houses with flowering branches. Maying ritualized the experience of spring and ensured that, even while wilderness retreated from advancing civilization, Americans would still venture from village, town and city; make contact with nature; and bring some back.

People looked forward to Maying as much as to spring itself. Thoreau, in his March 2 1859 journal, wrote, "We talk about spring as at hand before the end of February, and yet it will be two good months, one sixth part of the whole year, before we can go a-maying." John Muir, enduring an April 30th snow-storm on Mount Shasta in 1877, sought to lift his companion's spirits: "But never mind…; the night will wear away at last, and to-morrow we go a-Maying, and what camp fires we will make, and what sun baths we will take!" Charles J. Peterson in 1843 urged his readers, "Oh! Let us go a maying. We will away from the dull, brick-town; we will away into the country, the fresh, green, breezy country…. All through the long winter months we have been waiting for this day."

The month of May is named for Maia, a Roman springtime goddess. The first record of "Maying" was in Malory's 1485 *Morte d'Arthur*. Queen Guenever, accompanied by her knights and their ladies, all dressed in green, "rode on Maying in woods and meadows as it pleased them, in great joy and delight," ending up "bedashed with herbs, mosses and flowers, in the best manner and freshest."

The essence of Maying was always that physical bonding with nature, a shedding of adult inhibitions in celebration of the youth, innocence and beauty of spring and of love, abandon and loss of innocence. Maying, like childhood, partook of both wildness and innocence. In 1901 Dr. Charles C. Abbott wrote of the appropriate frame of mind for Maying: "There must be wildness in the air and we must feel it…In what consists this wildness? It may be asked. In everything. May is not a savage but she is wild. She is a child of Nature, and only such are free from all we would forget when we go a-Maying." The "Mayer" approaching the woods "indulges in mild delirium…. He feels like an escaped lunatic."

Indeed do we not feel madly liberated, as spring bursts upon us in delirious abandon? Trees just weeks ago bare now brim with color. The woods are carpeted with flowers: delicate sprays of toothwort; pink lined spring-beauties; starry white bloodroot; nodding yellow trout lilies; bluebells that ring bluer than blue; naughty yellow Dutchmen's breeches; shy ground-hugging trailing arbutus; spritely spikes of Canada mayflower; stately jack-in-the-pulpit; hepatica, anenome, and violets galore. Bees and butterflies dash blossom to blossom, humming and buzzing and fluttering.

All that activity, all that newness, all that life-affirming newborn sensual wildness – what do we *do* with it? It's human instinct to do *something*, to connect with the world by taking action. Our forebears knew what to do.

Spring

They'd go a-Maying. Dressed in green, bedecked by blooms, they'd become the flowering plants that defined spring.

The disappearance of Maying as a tradition – as a very *word* – leaves a void: one filled, inevitably, by commerce. What can we do with our spring fever but go to a garden center and buy mulch?

Reading these writers of a century or so ago using a word that has lost its meaning is like discovering a trunk of toys that let us play again. Oh, *that's* what I can do.

It's time to go a-Maying again. It's free. It's fun. It's all about flowers. Go out to woods and meadows, gather some flowers, wear them in your hair, or better yet, adorn your friend's hair. Indulge in some wild delirium.

Cautionary footnote: Ironically, before the tradition of gathering wildflowers in May was forgotten, there were *more* flowers growing in *more* places than there are today. So…. to make sure the flowers will outlive this reborn tradition, we must temper our delirium with a dewdrop of reason. Gather flowers in rights of way, not in protected parks; pick only where they're abundant, and don't take more than your share – indeed, one symbolic flower can represent all the others. Consider gathering flowers with camera or crayon. Let every flower loose a creative thought for honoring its existence.

Mother of Us All

On Mother's Day, life retells its story.

It all began with water, and on this Mother's Day the fog wafts in, settling over the world like an exhaled breath.

Hush. Out of respect for maternal sensibilities, the noisy machinery of human existence has been muffled. The usual pounding compressors and ringing hammers emanating from the construction site across the street have the day off. Lawn mowers and leaf-blowers are still. The morning is mercifully free of the usual roar and clatter of semis gearing down as they descend the nearby highway: even truck drivers have mothers today.

Into the fog-wrapped silence, birdsong weaves a jeweled raiment of music. The house wren cannot contain itself, song spills out like water from an overturned bucket. The indigo bunting steps carefully down the scale, while the northern parula warbler buzzes excitedly up it. The red-eyed vireo never tires of repeating his simple three-note inverted phrases; the wood thrush gives out with his extended trilling cadenza only when he pleases. The oriole whistles while he works, his mate listening quietly by his side: surely that piping accompaniment lightens their common toil.

Even the busiest, most distracted of mothers has time to listen to the concert today, and what a glorious consonance of events it is. The second Sunday in May coincides with the typical peak of spring avian migration. Birds are arriving by the cloudload from the South. The travelers mingle with year-round residents, who are busy building nests, foraging, and feeding their young. There are so many birds that it seems like the world cannot hold them all; they take turns coming down to earth.

Birds are not merely creatures of our time, they are also living links to a younger world, when the dominant life form was dinosaurs. Millions of years ago, the big, lumbering SUV-sized dinosaurs died out, but the small, nimble, airborne varieties had staying power. On this day, these feathered throwbacks are in constant motion: hopping, flitting, whirring, scratching, pecking, always flying, flying, flying.

On the wing, birds hunt other winged creatures – insects, a life-form even older than the dinosaurs. When ancient waters receded, arthropods were the first successful land-dwelling creatures. Their variety and adaptability enabled this group of organisms to spread all over the earth and colonize virtually every type of environment. In any particular season their relative abundance depends on local conditions. For entomologists and entomophages, the coming year will be a very good one. Weeks ago, rain drenched the world daily, providing extensive breeding grounds for flies, beetles, butterflies, spiders and other arthropods. Ending a seemingly endless drought, this soggy season has released an unaccustomed flood of multi-legged life. Surfaces are filled with crawling, scurrying life; water is beclouded with it; air is speckled with it.

Those same spring rains that nurtured the bugs also gave us an unaccustomed explosion of green. The earth is adorned from head to toe in leaves, from fine-textured grass on the woodland floor, to thick belts of shrubs, to leaf-trimmed tree hats. Before there were birds, before there were bugs, there were photosynthetic plants. The green cell – the one that uses the burnished coin of sunlight to change air and water into pent-up, packaged power – has been around longer than any of us. It is our common ancestor. And when it appeared on the scene, the green cell was a revolutionary.

In May, leaves bear the shiny bright sheen of youth, nourished by rain and fed by air. They turn expectant faces to the sun, ready to change the world with their energy. The tender young ones are miniature replicas of the mature forms they will turn into. From a low-hanging branch, waving leaves beckon to me. I bury my face in the foliage. Their clean fresh scent surrounds me, their fine soft texture tickles my face. I laugh with delight. It feels like the kiss of a newborn baby.

I Feel a Song Coming On

Why do birds sing in May?

Easy answer number one: to establish territory.

Easy answer number two: to attract a mate.

Easy (though hard-to-prove) answer number three: because they like to make music.

All true, but not, fundamentally, the answer.

Birds sing in May because the woods are full of green leaves.

If you're a birder – especially if you're a birder who needs officially sanctioned identification of the species you observe – there is comfort in knowing that a heard bird is as good as one you've seen, to the American Ornithologists' Union. Let's say you're in the woods and you hear a whistled "ta-wit ta-wit ta-wit tee-yo!" You can safely check off "hooded warbler" on your list, even though the only bird you've actually seen through the dense leaves is the one adorning the logo of your rather-useless-in-May binoculars.

If you're a bird, there is comfort in knowing that the species you've identified as (say) a fellow hooded warbler is singing from way over there: far enough away that he won't intrude onto your territory. Despite your distinctive colors, if you didn't hear him you wouldn't be able to see him through the dense underbrush. You might waste a lot of time setting up shop when in the next blackberry bush over, he's already staked his claim. Indeed, if you're a hooded warbler, you recognize the unique individual song of your neighbor from the previous year, when both of you staked out the same territory as you've done this year.

Too, if you're a bird, you sing here because you've stopped here, and you've stopped here because the woods are full of green leaves. The green leaves are being eaten by caterpillars, inchworms and other insect larvae. The larvae are eating because they were born into this life to eat leaves, and lucky for them they were born at a time of year when the green leaves are tender and abundant – although when their luck runs out, it's a bird that benefits. The green leaves feed the larvae, and the larvae – as well as the adult insects they grow into – feed the birds. And that is something to sing about.

If you're a bird, and you stopped here, and you're eating what's eating the leaves, there are enough leaves on the shrubs and trees for you to hide your nestlings from predators. And there are enough leaves to provide the shrubs and trees with energy through the end of the growing season, and even to enable them to store up a surplus: enough so they can emerge from dormancy in early spring, pushing leaf buds out while you're winging your way up from the south again. It's worth singing all summer long about that.

So, if you're like me, and you're walking in the woods one May morning – a good thick woods, with lots of understory trees like cherry and beech, and middle layer shrubs like blackberry, viburnum, and spicebush – and you hear a chirpy "ta-wit ta-wit ta-wit tee-yo," you will look in vain for the little yellow bird with a black monk's cowl perched somewhere oh so close, behind this leaf or that one or that one or over there. "Betcha betcha betcha can't see me," he sings. No, I don't see you. Or your nest, sitting a few feet above ground, which your mate has cleverly camouflaged with an outer surface of dead leaves and leaf skeletons. Good thing the woods were full of green leaves last year.

It's enough to make you burst into song. "Lovely-lovely-lovely-leaf-o!"

Wrong is Right

What's wrong with this picture? At first glance it's a tender scene of parental care. On the ground under the bird feeder, a newly fledged bird leans forward, quivering its wings, and opens its beak for Papa cardinal to drop in a sunflower seed. But … isn't the young cardinal a little – odd looking? Usually the juvenile looks like a female cardinal: variegated red and brown with a little crest like a cowlick. This one is buffy gray, streaked on the breast, round-headed; its beak is stout, but not oversized and triangular like that of a proper cardinal. Papa drops another seed into Junior's wrong-shaped beak, then flies off. Mama arrives.

46

Surely she'll recognize the error? A mother can tell! No, Junior gets his treat. Though Mama does seem a tad brusque.

As well she might. Being a parent is enough work without having someone else's offspring foisted upon you. This bird didn't look like a cardinal because *it wasn't a cardinal.* It was a brown-headed cowbird. Cowbirds don't even bother to build their own nests; there's no need, since they lay their eggs in other birds' nests. The unwitting host parents incubate the egg, tend the nestling and raise it as one of their own. Often the cowbird eggs hatch earlier than do the hosts' own young, so they get the most attention (and thus, food). The cowbirds' strategy of "brood parasitism" transfers to the host birds the energy cost of feeding and raising the hatchlings.

It doesn't seem right. The cowbird takes advantage of the host bird's natural parenting instincts, and hijacks them for its own purposes, in the process making it harder for the host to reproduce. In human terms, it's sleazy. We can applaud adoption, or foster parenthood. Even – more controversially – surrogate motherhood. But forced parenthood by deception? An abomination.

If brood parasitism offends the human moral standard, what about the strategy employed by bee flies, in the family Bombyliidae (pronounced bomb-bi-LYE-i-dee)? With its round brown fuzzy body and bouncing scientific name, the bee fly is the cuddly teddy bear of flies. It looks and sounds like a bumblebee (family Bombidae), but its flight patterns readily distinguish it from its namesake. A bumblebee flies slowly, forward or sideways, browsing from flower to flower like a fussy produce market patron, sensing shape, color and fragrance and finally slipping its whole bumbly self into the blossom. A bee fly, by contrast, doesn't so much fly as dart, dip and hover, in the manner of a hummingbird. With its long straight proboscis, it behaves like the bird, too, sipping nectar from deep within flowers without landing on them. Emerging in our area by late April, and remaining active on warm days through mid-May, the bee fly can be seen not only flying and feeding, but also basking in sunny spots to raise its internal temperature.

Cute, entertaining, doesn't bite – it certainly belongs on a "top ten" list of watchable wildlife. And yet…the bee fly can also be seen hovering over a small depression in the soil, moving the lower half of its body back and forth as if sweeping the doorstep. In a sense, that is what it's doing. This is the female bee fly's way of depositing eggs into the foyer of a ground-nesting solitary bee. The bee has dug a nest by tunneling into the loose soil. It is into this burrow that the bee places her egg. She busily gathers protein-packed pollen and energy-filled nectar, provisioning these stores in her nest for the larva to eat when it hatches, and finally she seals the tunnel entrance. All this preparation goes for naught. The bee fly, who has done none of the hard work of building a nest or gathering food, simply bowls its egg in while the bee is out foraging, then departs to continue living the high life: basking and flitting and supping. The bee completes her work none the wiser. When the bee fly egg hatches, it eats the bee larva's food supply and then (horrors!) eats the bee larva itself. It doesn't seem right.

Is it more wrong to be direct? The tobacco hornworm, a common vegetable-garden visitor, matures into a handsome orange-spotted brown sphinx moth with a nearly five-inch wingspan. It's a large smooth green caterpillar that doesn't have white projections. Doesn't, you say? Well, what are all those white rice-grain–like projections covering the smooth green surface? Ah, those are the cocoons of the braconid wasp. This wasp doesn't search out someone else's nest to lay its eggs in. It goes right to the source – the food source, that is. It injects its eggs into the hornworm itself (either the tobacco hornworm or the similar tomato hornworm). The eggs hatch into larva, which eat their way through the caterpillar to the surface, where they pupate; by the time they are ready to hatch … let's just say the world is poorer by one sphinx moth.

Parasites are deceivers, moochers, home invaders, and child-killers. What they do is not right, is it? Judging others' behavior and placing it into a moral framework is ingrained, if not instinctive, behavior, so it's only natural to apply it to the creatures who co-inhabit our home planet.

St. Anthony of Padua famously preached to the fishes, who appeared to appreciate his sermon, gathering in great numbers along the riverbanks below his impromptu pulpit. In "Des Antonius von Padua Fischpredigt," a German folk poem about the incident, we hear "Die Predigt hat g'fallen. Sie bleiben wie alle." (The sermon has pleased them. They remain unchanged.)

Some (including Mahler, who set the poem to music) interpret the poem as an ironic commentary on humankind's hypocrisy and capacity for self-delusion. But it could also be said that both the preacher and his listeners were right. "The sermon having ended, each turns himself around; the pikes remain thieves, the eels, great lovers." Of course, though the poem doesn't mention it, St. Anthony remained a devout monk. Whether you're a fish or a monk, appreciating the incomprehensible Other doesn't require any internal change. It's not wrong to pass judgment on the parasites, as long as we realize we are only judging ourselves when we do it.

Golden Locks and Red Sox

...in which it is revealed why a *Dandelion* is like Carl *Yastrzemski*...

Now, Dear Reader, you may well scoff at the premise and note, with a bored sigh, that both the dandelion and the baseball seasons encompass not only the summer but also large portions of spring and fall. And the wave of your hand indicates that you have observed that both of my Subjects light up a greensward, much to the delight (or consternation) of the lord and lady of the manor (depending on their inclination). With a shrug, you note that each remains in one place for an entire career, the dandelion being reliant on a taproot; the player, on the force of loyalty. All true enough, but mere spokes in the wheel, not the nub of the relation.

Exposing the obscure bond between the field-filler and the outfielder begins with a question that has a seemingly simple answer. Why are dandelions yellow? To anyone who has observed bees surveying a field, tracing S-paths and loop-de-loops, spotting a blossom and running straight for the target, the answer is obvious: dandelions are yellow because bees like yellow. More than yellow, they like the nectar of which the yellow is a reliable indicator. And further, though we are insensitive to these matters, dandelion yellow is not just yellow, it has a high reflectance coefficient for Ultraviolet light: when the sun is shining, a flowerhead in a sea of green (lawn or meadow) is the equivalent of torchlight at midnight to a flying insect. Drawn to the beacon, bees, flies, butterflies ants, beetles, and thrips plunge into its source to gather nectar. But it is all a sweet swindle: nectar is the bait, the pollinator the dupe, and the real story, the one you must know by heart, Dear Reader, is the transfer of pollen — which, attached ever-so-lightly to the stamen, detaches when brushed by a passing insect, thence carried by the unwitting bearer to another flower's stigma, fertilizing the flower.

But (you would be right to inquire) which flower? The dandelion pate supports a headdress of yellow plumes, each a flower in its own right — a floret. Between a hundred and two hundred florets huddle together in a flowerhead. Each floret is a graceful pinnate adornment. From an elliptical immature seed a single yellow five-lined petal arcs back, a tube that gradually opens up and flattens out toward the top. Around its base wave white filaments, like soft down. The yellow stigma emerges from the tubular portion of the petal and stands straight up, a "y" with two arms curling back inwards toward the stalk, like an elaborately-worked hairpin. Pollen grains, in matching yellow, bedeck the stalk. Any insect combing through the coiffure may transfer some pollen from one floret to another, either within the same flowerhead or between distinct flowerheads.

Would that it were so simple. The dandelion, not content with the standard story, need not depend on the wanderings of organisms that inhabit a separate branch of the tree of life. No, the dandelion could dispense with the come-hither yellow and the expensive libations provided to flying guests. It may self-pollinate, the pollen of a floret fertilizing its own seed. But even unfertilized, a dandelion floret can reproduce all by itself; this method of reproduction (called apomixis) is the equivalent of self-cloning in that the progeny are genetically identical to the parent. So the dandelion can take advantage of the benefits of sexual reproduction (adding genetic variability to the dandelion population) and of asexual reproduction (continuity of the successful individual).

Thus the dandelion game exalts both the individual and the team; tradition and novelty. Not dissimilar from baseball, you note? True, true – but no, reader, it is not yet time to head for the aisles; the Yaz connection remains unrevealed.

After blooming, the flowerhead closes for several days, then opens, transformed into a white globe , a ball of filaments: the seedhead. Each thread has a parachute-like canopy at the outer end and an achene (a one-seed-bearing fruit) at the inner end. Wind, heat or a puff of breath breaks the filaments free and the seeds are off. They scatter across the ground, not at all unlike the way a baseball player scatters hits around a field.

But the dandelion has another trick. Lest any plant find itself without pollinators for its flowers, or even without any flowers at all – victim of a mower, a weeder, or a grazer – all is not lost. Not content with pollination (self- or insect-enabled) and apomixis to reproduce, the dandelion also exploits vegetative propagation. The root, or even pieces thereof, will grow into a new plant.

Not one, not two, but three strategies. So the golden tiara that the dandelion wears ought, by rights, to be a triple crown. Not unlike that worn by the last pro baseball player to top the league in batting average, runs batted in, and home runs, the reigning royal standard-bearer, Mr. Yastrzemski.

Truly a Hall-of-Famer.

To See the World in a Grain of Pollen

As often as I can in springtime, I try to go out of my way to arrange an intimate encounter with a tree.

Trees are the largest life forms that most of us will ever meet up close. They tower over us and reach invisibly underneath, usurping the sky above and ground below. Their scale can be intimidating. And en masse, they invite awe. Atop the canopies of forest interiors, tree branches soar like cathedral trusses, inviting introspection and contemplation.

But where trees need not grow only straight and tall to reach the light, they meet us at our own height. Lining mountain streams and reaching out from the woods' edge, standing solitary watch in old fields, guarding parking lots and shading the middle school softball team's grandparents, trees extend their branches like welcoming arms.

Here the catkins reach down low enough to touch – to run your hand through, or bury your face in. The flowers skip across your skin like tiny dancers, tingling and tickling. Strands of red silk, strings of tawny pearls, spikes of jade-yellow fuzz: maple, oak and willow flowers feel as different as they look, shimmering, fluttering, dipping in the sun-heated breeze.

As the wind blows, the air fills with millions upon millions of investments – almost all of which end up lost. Each catkin is a flower studded with florets, and each floret holds a cache of pollen that it casts into the air. Breathe in. Whether you seek out a spring fling with a tree or, like my son, prefer to trim a clothes tree in season, if you are alive to inhale, you can't help but have your own close encounter with a tree.

Of all these innumerable pollen grains, most miss their mark, and a great many of those lodge in eyes, throats and lungs, where their journey ends with a sneeze. If you're unfortunate enough to be hypersensitive to pollen, their presence will trigger an immune response, escalating the mild, irritated sneeze to a histamine-fueled battle that does neither trees nor humans any good. This is intimacy of a different order, but a necessary implication of the system that trees have devised to spread their kind as far as possible. Allergies are collateral damage in a tree's empire-building campaign.

For these great beings depend, as equally as do the smallest of us, on minute packages of genetic material for their reproduction. Throwing caution to the wind, a grain of tree pollen launches from the male catkin with only the remotest hope of accomplishing its mission. Somewhere out there is a sticky female flower. On maples, it dresses in brazen red; on oaks it hides shyly in the crook of the leaf bud; on willows, it hides in plain sight on catkins nearly identical to the male flowers. In the unlikely event that one of the billions of pollen grains lands on a stigma, and that the female accepts the pollination offer (usually, a tree rejects not only its own pollen, but also the pollen of other species), fertilization will follow.

Of course that doesn't end the story; the seeds or nuts produced by fertilization still have to be dispersed, germinate and grow to maturity – a process that the tree has no control over. It depends instead on wind, water, and even autonomous agents such as seed-eating or nut-caching animals.

The odds against any single pollen grain developing into a tree that reproduces itself are astronomical. Is this a system that any rational being would have devised?

An encounter with a tree flower is a glimpse into the madness that binds the unmerciful randomness of the universe together into what we call hope. This is the grand unifying force. No wonder its touch tingles, like electricity.

Stop the World

In the symbolic language we use to process experience, elements of the natural world are freighted with meaning. Water represents constant change. The sky stands for unpredictability. The earth that we walk on, however, is solid certainty. Land is the base on which we stand, the bottom – in Latin, the fund. This metaphor becomes the way in which we characterize what we know. An illogical assertion is said to be *groundless*; truths are *fundamental*. Oh yes, we say, there is substance to that claim. When fate deals us a blow we shake our fists at the heavens, and stamp our feet on the earth in defiance, as if to say, you can't take this away from me. This I know.

Yet the world we stand on, which seems so solid, is in fact a shifting tiramisu pudding, a melange of organic and inorganic matter composed of mismatched grains and bits and chunks layered on top of bedrock. What's more, it is full of holes. The spaces between bits of matter hold air and water, those oh-so-changeable elements. Frost heaves are manifestations of the spongecake-like nature of our "solid" earth: during winter the water in these holes freezes, expands and lifts the soil surface right up.

So the good old reliable top layer that we stand on with such confidence ought to slide right off the face of the earth, slip from the upper crust that it coats like a skin on the pudding. In early spring, it seems about to do just that. Water saturates the upper level of soil as it unfreezes. Snowbanks melt and most new precipitation now falls as rain. It is mud season. But typically, and tellingly, mud appears only in disturbed areas – places like cleared lands, eroded hillsides, and trails. Places where the top layer is bare earth, stripped of its plants.

What keeps the face of the earth from sliding off its rocky bone structure are roots: plunging tree roots, spreading shrub roots, tenacious grass roots, multitudinous wildflower roots. How *fortunate* we are that the growing season for wildflowers coincides with the season for mud! No, it is much less *fortune* than a matter of survival. Were it not for all those filaments, those tendrils spreading in a subsurface net, spring's torrents would drive the soil down to the oceans, gusting winds would blow it away. Our landscape, shorn of soil, would resemble the barren rocks of the Mediterranean, or the deserts of North Africa – landscapes where loss of vegetation, whether induced by human means or climate change or both, was not the result, but the cause, of the change from their former Edenic state as lush forests. Trees beget trees, in a bed of soil.

Along the North Branch of the Neshaminy Creek as it wends its way into Peace Valley Park in New Britain Township, Bucks County, the stream bank rises nearly vertically in a small half-gorge. At the bottom, the soil has been eroded over time, torn off by rain and flood. It is as if a knife had sliced into the bank and cut straight down, leaving a steep-fronted wall between four and eight feet high. This affords a cross-section view of the forested hillside, one that normally lies hidden beneath layers of soil. Jutting out from the bank are tree roots bent into right angles, jammed in like hooks into a pegboard. Their form is the record of years of struggle, holding back the relentless tide of shifting rock and soil. Below them, old matted roots, caked with sediment, hang along the banks in a continuous undulating curtain, following the line of the ground as it dips and rises. Behind the curtain is the drama that goes on year after year. The soil moves, it cannot help itself. The roots grab hold, they hold back. Here, they say. Here is where I have chosen to make a home. What the roots hold back, stays in place. It becomes the familiar solid surface that we like to think of as terra firma.

Wild Beauty

In early spring, imported, cultivated bulbs such as crocus and narcissus bring a riot of incandescent purple, orange and yellow into the garden. Native to Turkey and Armenia, and cultivated primarily by Dutch growers, they respond extraordinarily well to the mid-Atlantic climate. They get planted next to mailbox posts and under foundation shrubs. These flowers have come to symbolize spring, even though many of them start to bloom in winter. Every year, too, it seems that they get knocked down by a belated blast of snow or ice.

Most of our native spring wildflowers, by contrast, wait until it is unlikely they'll be iced over, then poke tentative heads up out of moist, woodsy soil. These ephemerals bloom just as the threat of winter weather has receded, and fade before trees and shrubs bear leaves large enough to block the sun. Whereas the upstart imports bear flowers defiantly out of proportion to their stems, aptly named spring beauties are a pale pinkish white with delicate half-inch-wide flowers nodding just off the ground. The spring beauty's companions include the toothwort, which has slightly larger white bell-shaped flowers drooped over deeply notched tripartite leaves; and the bloodroot, whose bright white waxy blossoms, easily a match for crocuses in size, open only for a day or two, while the round gray-green leaves persist for months.

Look closely at the spring beauty and you see that the pink color is imparted primarily by thin pink lines radiating from the center. These are the guidelines, literally, that pollinating insects follow in order to get to the nectar at the conjunction of the petals. Bees and ants emerge hungry from their hives when winter lethargy wears off; the flowers are a sweet spring tonic.

I plan and plant Dutch bulbs, selecting a varied, yet harmonious palate, choosing locations for the maximum visual impact, and arranging a mix of sizes and forms. Yet I also wait impatiently for the unplanted flowers to bloom where they may. I find spring beauties and their associates scattered all over my yard, a hillside haven for mature oak, hickory and walnut trees.

Chemicured turf lawns are replacing vast stretches of rich soil in our area, and invasive, opportunistic exotic plants are moving in to the remainder. So there are fewer and fewer places allotted to the spring beauty – few enough that although it is not considered a rare plant, the guidebooks nevertheless admonish foragers to gather the edible roots only where it is abundant or the need is critical.

Spring

I have, however, found spring beauties lurking in the margins of my gravel driveway, advancing from their positions under the surrounding trees in anticipation of the day they can stake their claim without being ground into oblivion. Because that day has not yet arrived, I dig them up, gently, and move them to a wet spot in the yard where I have raked out clumps of aggressive lesser celandine, an import that spreads rapidly in wet places. This spot lies over a seep and its black soil contrasts with the predominant red clay. I water the new arrivals and watch over them. They seem to take to their new home quite well.

Does planting these wild things make them, somehow, less wild? Next year, should they come up again, will knowing that I put them there lessen my delight in finding them? Why should it be different that a human deliberately put down a plant, rather than the seeds having been thrown by the wind or carried by an ant? Does treating the Earth as a garden fundamentally alter the way we relate to ecosystems, by further tightening the screws of our dominion over the planet? I am gratified by knowing that in both a micro and a macro sense I am doing good works by helping – even in such a small way – to perpetuate a species and sustain a part of a system. But I am also sad at feeling that I need to save a form of life that has not had to depend on me, or any other human, to thrive, until now.

Eventually, unless we leave room in the world for the wild, it will cease to exist. My hope is that by planting these flowers I make it more likely for them to survive until we get wise to that idea. We need not to be needed.

In the meantime, it is spring, and they are still here, and they are beautiful.

I Know Where the Bees Went

Last night I dreamed of them, dreamed of pillowing my head on their soft quilted white blossoms, dreamed of their scent curling around me as into its arms, drawing me up, up, up. till I didn't want to come back down.

I awoke in a fever, driven with yearning, driven to find the flowers of the honey locust.

Green leaves line the streets. Green leaves rim the fields. Green leaves crowd the banks.

Where are the locust trees? Where are the waterfalls of white froth cascading down over the canopy, the oval leaflets peering out like eyes through a veil? Where oh where are my locusts? There's one! – It's out of reach. Should I risk falling? Another! On someone's property. Should I risk arrest? There! Too close to traffic. Should I risk death?

One here. One there. Why not whole groves of them? Native though they are, farmers in this area used to plant locust trees. The old ones knew that the bees would find the trees. And where there are bees, there is the land of milk and honey ...and locust honey is the most exquisite honey of all, the fruit of dazzling desire.

Where are the bees? They say the honeybees have left their hives, and won't come back. They've disappeared. All kinds of theories abound. Maybe something is killing them off. A new virus, a new fungus. Pesticides, perhaps. Or cell phones. Maybe something is affecting their homing instincts.

There! A grove, a fencerow, a thick stand of black locusts, just where they ought to be, across route 202 from the hospital. Here they are, ready to give sweet therapy, cure the ills of all, nurse the sick back to health and transport the healthy to earthly paradise.

The flowers hang in clusters, like grapes. The fragrance is sweet and hopelessly, helplessly perfumed of everything that anyone could ever have wanted. I breathe it in and can't stop inhaling.

Bees above and bees below, parting the petals. As with other members of the pea family, locust flowers are arranged like little bonnets, with two half-round petals behind and two crescents protruding perpendicularly from the middle, protecting a horn-shaped fifth petal that is the object of the bee's devotion.

The aroma of heavy, honeyed ease envelopes me. I swoon, covered in blossoms. This is the stuff that dreams are made of. I awake, in the middle of the night, surrounded by flowers. They still exude their honeyed scent in the dark. The leaves have gone to sleep: exhausted, they fold into themselves. But the flowers can't help it; they keep perfuming the night air, as if the bees might still come to them. Or as if the bees were not the point at all. As if the point were the perfume itself, the heady, addicting, overwhelming expression of the sweetness of life -- and the bees merely hopelessly, helplessly intoxicated by its power.

Where are the bees? Gone to flowers, every one. Looking, looking, looking for the locust.

I will follow them.

Summer

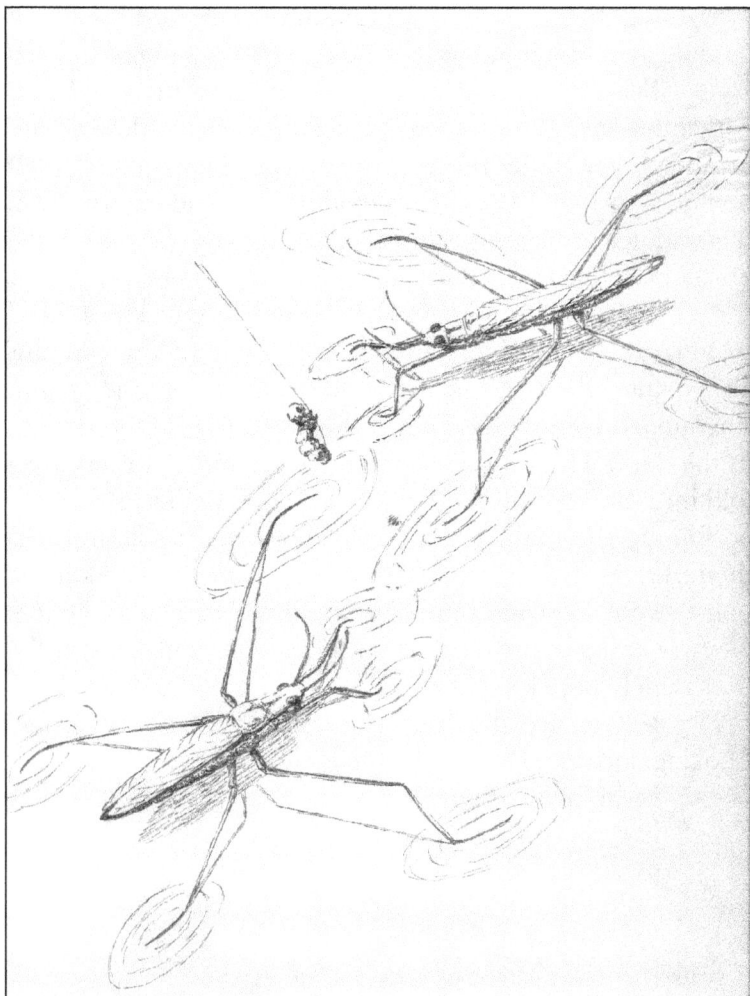

Dealing with Forever

The best definition of forever that I ever heard was "after our lifetime." It's not very poetic, but doesn't it state the least we can hope for?

That's what Charles and Mae Coiner must have had in mind when they donated their 108-acre Coltsfoot Farm in Buckingham Township, Bucks County, to the Natural Lands Trust in 1985. The couple had no children, but they did have a piece of land they had worked and lived on for decades and they did not want it to die with them. The arrangement allowed them to enjoy their property for the rest of their lives; then the Trust would take full title to it.

For almost five years now, the Coiners' land has been in the hands of the Trust. The new owners renamed it the "Paunacussing Preserve" after the small, yet vital, creek that courses through it. The state classifies the Paunacussing Creek as "high quality/cold water fishery," and Bucks County identifies the creek as an important natural area.

One fine day in August, Jim Thompson, the Preserve's affable resident manager, gave me a tour of the site. Just over half is being farmed; the rest is in varying stages of natural succession. We ambled through the shady yard of the fieldstone farmhouse, by a brick-lined herb garden, along the remains of a fenced pasture gone to seed, between rows of corn, around a pond, across a meadow, down a streamside trail, and through unmarked woods.

In the woods, we stepped carefully through muck that caked our shoes. Channels snaked lazily around tree roots, connecting puddles that dotted the forest floor. We knelt beside one pool, barely three inches deep and no more than few feet around. Just as we bent down, a frog jumped in. Clouds of mud billowed up from the bottom. When the cloud settled, the pool became clear again, and there, in the center, was a column of bubbles, rising from a navel-sized opening in the bottom.

This tiny spring, one of many scattered around the Preserve, is part of the headwaters of the Paunacussing. Before the creek empties into the Delaware at Lumberville, before it rushes down rocky slopes, before it wends its way under stone bridges and behind old stone houses in Carversville – before it is a creek, it is uncounted puddles, channels and rivulets, all fed by springs. These headwaters create cool temperatures and provide a constant source of nutrient-filled groundwater: conditions amenable to abundant and diverse stream life. Eliminate the headwaters, and the creek might still flow, especially during storms when runoff pours into it. But it would be lifeless: a drainage ditch, fit only to carry water out of the way. So these perforations in the earth are a big part of why the Preserve is worth preserving.

Now that the Natural Lands Trust has sole responsibility for this property, what should they do? How – if at all – do they maintain the historic balance between agricultural and natural lands? What should be planted, and what weeded out? Should herbicides be used? Should the pond stay or go? How to keep deer from clear-cutting new growth? And what about people – are they welcome, or are they inherently a destructive element?

The Trust is just starting to wrestle with these questions. The answers will shape the way the site looks, which species will thrive here, and the extent to which the creek can continue to bubble up in the woods. There will be consequences in the near term, to be sure. Some could be significant. But the Trust can afford to try things, see what works, and even make mistakes. They intend to hold on to this property for a long time. As Jim Thompson put it: "We're dealing with forever here."

Oh yes, forever. How long is that?

Look at it this way: We are the Coiners' forever.

In the Shade Pool

Shade is what is left of sunlight when the tree is finished using it. Light slips through the spaces between leaves, and between cells in the leaves; it bounces off leaftops and branches and leafbottoms and back down again. The tree takes as much of the light as it can and lets the rest go. At the tree's base, the dregs of light collect. We are bottom-feeders of light; we revel in the muck of the shade pool.

On a summer day, the heat is thick and suffocating, the light is blinding. This light is not for us. We can't use it; we toast and burn, sweat and steam. Step into the shade and breathing comes easier, eyes need not squint. It is cool here, the kind of cool that no awning or umbrella can duplicate. The leafy canopy deflects direct heat before it can penetrate; air under the canopy still slowly heats up, but it rises and curls around the leaves, escaping. Look out from the shadespace to the brightness beyond; it shimmers as if seen from underwater.

There may be forty Eskimo words for snow, but we dwellers in the Eastern woodlands know there are nearly as many kinds of shade: dry, dense, dappled, deep, damp, light, open, medium, partial, full. Shade under a fragrant grove of white pines is fragile, its edges feathery, as if it could disappear at any moment. A maple-shaded brook lends moisture to the air; moss coats the rocks and hangs from the branches; the shade seems as ancient and unmovable as the sheet-flat rocks lining the streambed. Under the low sheltering branches of mountain laurels blooming with pink powderpuffs, shade is intimate, small-scaled like playing house; shade under a solitary oak in a field is heroic, monumental: surrounded by its opposite, it stands as much for the idea of shade as for the thing itself.

Sunlight can exist without shade. The converse is not true: shade is the needy one in this relationship. Steadfast and dependable, its riches there for the taking, sunlight is also imperious, knowing its supplicants can add nothing to its wealth. Shade craves attention, but on its own terms. A green leaf is the go-between, the facilitator, the matchmaker. Let there occur an opening in the canopy – caused by a lightning strike or a fire, or by a tree growing taller so that a single limb now arches higher than an adjacent one. A shaft of sun now pierces the veil of leaves. Photosensitive leaf cells signal the presence of sunlight; the tree grows toward it, then captures it. Shade closes over the sunlight like a wave over a sandcastle.

As a tidal pool lingers between high tides, a bit of the ocean left behind temporarily until the sea returns and reclaims it, a shade pool subsists between sunrise and sunset, a bit of night left behind until darkness reclaims it. Let a tree be your diving board – take the plunge.

The Untouchables

If ever a bird could be said to have cooties, it's the turkey vulture.

In flight, this large bird is awkward, rocking its six-foot wingspan back and forth as it seems to struggle to maintain its balance and stay aloft, all the while looking like it is just about to stall and drop straight down out of the sky. Up close, the adult's featherless red head, stuck atop a goony brownish-black body, draws your gawking attention the same way a car accident does: you just can't help but stare at the disaster. Once, on a memorable birding caravan trip, I precipitated a fender-bender by asking "what's that?" as we passed by a turkey vulture standing in a field. The driver turned to look, and rammed into the rear bumper of the vehicle ahead. It had no doubt stopped to enable the occupants to observe a much more interesting bird, perhaps a rare tropical migrant – certainly not the common turkey vulture.

On a hawk watch, where the objective is to count as many raptors as can be seen from one spot, birders sneer as they count "TVs." Even the nickname bespeaks contempt – what other bird shares its abbreviation with a mind-numbing appliance? In this setting, the vultures' graceless flight is accentuated, because they occupy the same airspace as the majestic eagles, the hurtling falcons and the soaring buteos and accipiters. Vultures, although they look and fly like hawks, are really in the stork family. Just like those misfits in elementary school, they seem oblivious to the fact that they just don't fit in.

No, this is one bird whose likeness will probably never adorn the logo of a nature organization. The sanitation engineers' association, though, would be appropriate. Carrion feeders, the vultures clean up roadsides littered with carcasses. The vulture's bald red head is well-adapted to its task, since the gore of its prey would get stuck in feathers if there were any around its head and neck. And, unlike hawks and owls who hunt live quarry, vultures don't need to be steady fliers with pinpoint accuracy: their prey has not moved for quite some time.

Vultures thrive where roads and wildlife meet – not along urban highways, which cross through areas where the nonhuman environment has all but been obliterated, but beside those bypasses, state routes and turnpikes that cut through rural farmland, exurbia and suburbia. Here there is a great enough density of both cars and animals to make it worthwhile for a vulture to cruise a regular route.

In Point Pleasant, Bucks County, on the Delaware River, there is a fortuitous combination of habitat. Here, near US Route 202, an endless stream of cars ferries commuters hurrying to their destinations, past farms and golf courses and housing developments. Here also are long rocky ridges that rise abruptly from both sides of the river's floodplain. Wind spills over the ridges, creating air currents that the birds ride along, their own highways paralleling the earthbound ones. Finally, here there are abundant woods and trees for roosting. Towards dusk the vultures float in along the ridgelines, slowly dropping lower and lower, circling in small groups before settling in for the night. They do not make noise, and their dark color blends in with the darkening sky, so the ground below – whitened from their droppings – may be the only clue to their presence.

There they sit, hunched in rows along the tree limbs, shifting occasionally from branch to branch and tree to tree as new arrivals alter the roosting status, while darkness falls. The nearby roads thrum with homebound traffic. Overnight, deer, possums, raccoons and skunks wander out in search of food: out of the nests, the dens, the burrows; out of the trees, the fields and the banks, and across the asphalt. At dawn, the rising sun gleaming off the hoods of cars reveals a roadside bounty.

The highway slices through the countryside. Off to the side, a vulture descends. It goes to work. Best not to look at it. It is an ugly bird, isn't it? Off to the side, flung out of our way, lie the mangled messes that we make of other lives. Best not to look while someone else cleans it up. Someone whose revolting appearance befits the task. Best not to look.

Katy Did It

The heat of an August day smothers sounds like a cotton earplug. As evening falls, the warmth draws away. A breeze fans the tree leaves. A single hickory nut falls onto the ground – tumm! As if signaled, cicadas in the trees wind up for a final buzzing crescendo and decrescendo, a long slow rhythm like a meditative breathing in and out, and then they are quiet.

Now the concert begins. Into the silence, the soft trilling of ground crickets lays out an airy, delicate foundation, like a lace doily. High in the trees, the true katydids begin singing, tentatively, singly, then in call and response: katydid, katydidn't. The sounds intersect and coalesce, break apart and converge. From shrubs lower to the ground, a sound like a dowel being scraped across a wooden ridged cylinder – the oblong-winged katydid's call

– intermittently punctuates the chorus. From the same vicinity, the round-winged katydid gives out a bleating rattle, pausing briefly, the way a snorer does. Assorted tree cricket songs – chains of chirps, some long, some short – filter down from above, underlining here, filling in the gaps there.

One note is insufficient for a song, one beat alone is not a rhythm. One katydid maketh not a summer's night. The polyrhythms of the night arise not from the songs of individual insects, but from the synchronizing of each song into a chorus. Like waves breaking upon a beach, the layers form and reform, intersect with a crashing roar, then die down. Crickets singing near each other follow a leader, so their choruses augment the individual voices into a mass. Katydids, on the other hand, time their calls so as to avoid synchronizing with an adjacent individual, so their choruses have a regular, two-part character.

As I sit motionless beneath the choir, the sound bounces from tree to tree above my head: a continuous rocking back and forth, back and forth, one-two, one-two. The rhythm of footsteps. I step out, walking down the road, under the arch of trees that are echoing katydid, katydidn't. As I gain speed, one-two, one-two becomes one-one, two-two, my motion blurring the beat, until I am in an open treeless space and the sound fades.

Moonrise, a smoldering coal suspended in the sky above, holds me in my tracks. Next to the Moon, Mars glows like a spark thrown off from the glowing ember. The waxing and waning of the Moon describes the rhythm of months. By the end of this month, Mars will be closer to Earth than it has been in 67,000 years. This is the rhythm of the universe, played out in time spans too large to be comprehended.

Within the long, slow pulse of the intersecting planetary orbits, which encircle the annual return of each season, which enclose the monthly circuit of the moon, which surrounds the daily rhythm of the earth turning from light to darkness, time passes. Now the heat of the day's sun is a memory; as night cools the air, the insect songs slow down, their pitch lowers. The slow cadence fills the air, throbs against the ground, and under my walking feet, one-two, one-two, and then into my heart. Ba-*dum*, ba-*dum*. Katy*did*, katy*didn't*.

Today's Model

Bright black googly headlamps, a long low pearly green midsection and upswept tail fins extending a body length and more behind. Under the gleam of the Mercedes dealer's bright lights it looked like a jeweled brooch. My son, the car maven, recognized it right off. A mayfly.

On this hot, humid late spring evening mayflies dotted the smooth reflective surfaces of the cars like chips in ice cream.

Mayflies are of the order ephemeroptera, meaning short-lived winged creatures, referring to their adult form. The immature mayfly nymphs live for a year underwater, attached to the underside of rocks in a stream, where they breathe through gills and feed on algae and other small plants. The nymphs crawl up to a surface to molt, in two stages, into the final winged adult form. During this last phase the mayflies mate and lay eggs, but they do not eat. There's no time for that. They have only a day or two to live.

So here were all these mayflies, just out of the water, having done all their mayfly business. Now they were spending their last hours on earth, sitting on a car under bright lights.

At least it was a luxury car.

But these mayflies ought to have been resting on rocks, or branches, in the cool shelter of a streambank; their wings, clear and brilliant, shining like mica in the moonlight. What is the quality of a life that plays out on an artificial surface, under artificial light, marking time until death?

So much of our lives are spent in environments of our own making. More than that, we force other creatures to exist in those same environments. Life is nothing if not adaptable, of course. Cliff-nesting swallows find bridge abutments to their liking; mosquitoes breed in abandoned tires; iron-eating bacteria thrive in discharge pipes. Our world becomes their world because they have no choice.

We have a choice. We can choose to impose, or we can choose to include. We can impose our world, constructed to fit our selfish needs, or we can include the needs of others in our designs. We can turn the lights off, leave the streambanks clear, shade the creeks and keep them unpolluted and free-running.

The presence of mayflies in a stream is an indicator that the stream is healthy, that it supports an ecosystem complex enough to support not only the mayflies and their food sources, but also the fish that feed on the mayflies, as well as the anglers who feed on the fish.

The presence of mayflies in a parking lot is not an indicator that the parking lot is healthy. It just indicates the presence of a nearby stream and lights bright enough to attract the insects. It also indicates that we still have a chance to include the needs of these creatures in our world. They are still with us, as they have been every year, unlike last year's car models. Next year? Well, don't go shopping for a Studebaker.

Wait and See

Normally, trees don't cheep. They may creak; they may rustle; but cheeping is not in their vocabulary. So, as I pass a snag in the woods, and hear a cheeping from twenty feet up, I stop to investigate.

It's a steady high-pitched chorus, each voice repeating one note over and over. By contrast, the repeated six-note phrase of the red-eyed vireo that is supplying the background music on this drowsy early summer afternoon – a song that I usually hear as monotonous – seems positively melodic. "Drink your tea? Drink your tea!" sings the vireo, hidden in the leaves of a nearby beech tree. "Eeep, eeep, eeep!" chirps the chorus, like the sound of a squeaky old motor, the kind you see nailed to a plank in a garage shop. To power that constant squeaking requires fuel, and there is no mistaking the sound of nestling birds begging for food high up in the tree.

The tree is dead, and dead straight for twenty feet, at which point it breaks off in a jagged crenellation. It has no branches to provide a crook for a twiggy home, no leaves hiding a mud-caulked grass nest. There are, however, three round holes in the trunk, each about two inches in diameter. The lowest one, maybe fifteen feet up, is roughly cut, with deep gashes around the edge, and is too shallow to serve as a habitation. The middle hole, though deep enough, has weathered to a uniform gray; it looks abandoned – as if the owners permanently retired to warmer climes. But the highest cavity looks crisp and clean around the edges, freshly cut and well-maintained. All evidence suggests that the parents will be back any minute now with provisions for the household.

So I wait.

Waiting is a state of *being* that is dominated by what *will be*. Waiting shifts back and forth between hope and fear, faith and doubt: two sides of the same lens that focuses the mental telescope on the future. To wait is to comprehend that the present becomes the future. But what to *do* while waiting?

Nestlings cheep.

Doing creates the future out of the present. For nestlings, cheeping leads to a well-fed future. The distinctive begging calls and gaping mouths of the young arouse the feeding instinct in the parents, who go off and forage. But the cheeping continues while the chicks wait in the nest. What is the point of this ceaseless cheeping, when parents cannot hear? It's not mere idle time-filling, but a strategy for erasing doubt. If a nestling anticipates the eventual return of the parents, yet has no way of knowing how far away they are, it must always act as if the feared future is about to happen. ("What if they come back and I'm not making any noise? Maybe they'll drop the tasty grasshopper and fly away.") Indeed, the more intense cheepers get more attention, and more food, than their siblings. So hungrier chicks, the ones who have not been fed as much in the past, beg more intensely. It takes more energy to do so, but not doing it would make things worse.

On the other hand, there is a form of waiting that consists of doing nothing. There is nothing I can do to make the parents come back, and much that I could do that would prevent them from returning. To create the future I hope for, I must be still.

Unceasing, unbroken cheeping from the tree. We've been waiting a good ten minutes, at least. Time enough for me to have observed a fly landing on an orb-weaver's web, a wasp depositing eggs into a leaf. The vireo's song seems more rapid now, so the temperature must have gone up.

"Peeek!"

Red splotch on the back of its head, black-and-white stripes across its back, a male downy woodpecker alights on a branch next to the dead tree. His feathers are ragged and his beak is a mess, with bits of grass stuck to it randomly. He looks around. If the cheeping can possibly get more insistent, it does. Papa woodpecker flies over to the topmost hole, sticks his head in. Loud, triumphant cheeping. He leaves, and a female takes his place, thrusting her splotch-less head into the nest. As she departs, a bird nearly climbs out after her, looking for more. The chestnut-colored stripe on the top of its head is the woodpecker equivalent of a freshman beanie, the mark of callow youth. *Bring the world to me.* For now, all its needs are fulfilled; for now, waiting is all that is required.

The adult pair come and go swiftly, taking turns, first one then the other, flying to nearby trees, poking under the bark, and returning with food. Three, four rounds, only brief intervals between.

Then they don't come back. Seconds pass. The cheeping is insistent. Seconds add up, and minutes go by.

It is hot.

Wait, wait. If not now, then.

Lunch Break

A titmouse, its back the deep blue of a newborn's eyes, breast the gray of the sky just before it snows, and its own eyes bright black beads, sat for an uncharacteristic moment on the birdfeeder perch. Usually it spent only as much time standing still as it took to grab a seed from our feeder. It flashed back and forth between the holly tree and the feeder, a few feet.

Tucked up in the tree where the branches emerge from the trunk, the titmouse would crack the seed it had just secured. Sometimes it would tap the branch too, looking for insects just beneath the bark.

You rarely see a lone titmouse. Typically, they travel in mixed flocks with chickadees, who are either black-capped, Carolina, or, most commonly in central Bucks County, a hybrid variety. Chickadees are easily recognized with their jaunty black hats and their "dee-dee-dee" call; titmice seem quieter in the winter than in the spring and summer when their "peter peter" calls fill the woods.

While chickadees seem almost tame, and can be easily trained to eat out of hand, the titmouse is not content to stand in one place long enough for you to become friends. So it was an unusual treat to be able to train the binoculars on one, for that moment. Suddenly, it was gone, back in the holly tree.

There was a whoosh, and a bird with a russet and white striped breast and huge yellow talons flew straight toward the window. A few feet in front of the window it turned 180 degrees and landed in the holly, where it sat. A sharp-shinned hawk.

Blue-jay sized, these woodland hawks are fast and quiet and can out-maneuver an F-16 any day. They're built for pursuing their prey – those same songbirds we feed through the winter – in and out of trees.

From the holly came frantic alarm calls. One bird per flock – usually the weakest – has the task of sounding the alarm. The one giving the alarm, of course, also attracts the attention of the predator. But someone has to do it.

The hawk sat – just sat – for a moment, no longer than the moment the titmouse had sat, but long enough to train the binoculars on it and appreciate its beauty: the fine lines on its breast the color of fallen oak leaves, the bold black stripes on its tail, its orange eyes like a setting sun. Then it propelled itself up and into the tree. There was a wild scrambling, branches shook and birds shot out; then the hawk emerged, with its prey in its talons. It dropped to the ground, and stood on the bird, pecking at it a few times. It was a titmouse. The little blue-gray bird moved a few times then no more. The hawk flew off, lunch grasped in its talons.

All was quiet.

A half hour later, blue wings flashed back and forth between the holly tree and the feeder.

It's risky out there. But a bird has to eat.

Play's the Thing

Given the human penchant for play, it's a wonder so few plants take advantage of it for their own purposes.

In the game of life, it helps to spread your offspring so as to give more of them a chance to succeed. Plants cannot move, so they rely on external agents to disperse their progeny. Typical strategies involve betting on someone, or something, to brush by seed pods that stick to fur and eventually fall off far away; or enticing some creature to eat seed-containing fruit so as to distribute them at – ahem – a later time. Then there are more subtle tactics. Oaks, for example, rely on the fact that squirrels do not eat all of the acorns that they bury: the leftovers sprout into new trees. If squirrels were more efficient, they would eat themselves out of a food supply.

If you have the right attitude, the world outside is an amusement park.

Children and dandelions seem made for each other. The lollipop-like seedheads explode so deliciously with a huff and a puff! Seeds scatter on the wind; you can watch an individual one sail up and down the air currents like a tiny paraglider. This globetrotting wildflower, prized for its taste in its native Europe, despised for its defiance of lawn borders in America, does not need the helping human breath to spread; wind power is sufficient. But what fun would there be in waiting for the wind?

Milkweed pods swell over the summer, eventually attaining an unmistakable gourd-like shape. When a seed pod is ripe, the fluff peeks out of a slit just wide enough for tiny fingers to push into and tear apart. The seeds can be set on their journey with a flick. In another place, a child may snatch the slow traveler from the air. "Make a wish!" goes the refrain. Eyes closed, one whispers the secret hope, then – to make it come true – lets the seed go. Clutched in an eager hand, is the seed wishing, too? The heart's desire: a warm bed, a sheltered home, some space to settle in and a cool drink.

Summer

The fun of playing with jewelweed is the delight of a surprise that you know is coming. You'll find jewelweed colonies in wet places: in moist woods, and in marshes, but also in drainage ditches. Their egg-shaped leaves partially hide the orange or yellow flowers that dangle like ornaments. Once the flower disappears, you have to look hard for the slender, half-inch-long seed case under the leaves, looking like a miniature peapod. There's only one way to tell if it's ripe, and that's to tap it. If it's ready, at the slightest touch the pod will detonate in a shower of seeds. Squealing is the only appropriate response. Why do they call this plant the "touch-me-not"? It must have been named by the same people who told you to turn off that racket you call music. These are the people who know that anything fun has to be dangerous.

For fun that partakes a bit of the dark side, one need go no farther than a woodsy lawn. Find the papery brown balls with a pinhole at the top. Find a stick. Then – whomp! Hit the puffball! The brown smoke that wafts out is a cloud of mushroom spores, gone forth to multiply. Some call the puffball "the devil's snuffbox." What the devil has to do with it is not at all obvious. This is a fairly harmless mushroom; it's edible when it first appears as white buttons in the spring, and is used in folk remedies for various maladies. But even the most peace-loving, angelic among us gets a devilish gleam in the eye when given the chance to pound on the little globes. Is the puff of smoke a hint of black magic? a touch of the mad scientist? No matter. You've done the deed. The puffball cares not for your motivation. Its children thank you.

The Weight of Water

Problem: calculate the weight of water. Show your work. Ten points each.

1) At Lenape Middle School in Doylestown, over 8.57 inches of rainfall were recorded in July 2004, almost twice the average precipitation for the month. That adds up to about 44.22 lbs. per square foot of surface area (the density of water is about 62.43 lbs. per cubic foot or 0.036127 per cubic inch), or 1,989,875.16 lbs. in an acre. That's about 167 elephants, or to use a measuring unit indigenous to our area, 444 Ford Explorers.

2) Lest they defoliate my plants, I knock Japanese beetles from shrubs into a bucket of water held under the leaves. No more than an inch or two of water is required, but on one occasion, I attempt to use the bucket when it's already full of rainwater. If you want to know the weight of water, try lifting a bucket of it. Don't have a bucket? Lift the nearest human. If it's a man, he is 60 percent water; a woman, 50 percent (the other 10 percent must be feminine intuition).

3) As reported by *The New York Times*: On the Qingdao beach by the Yellow Sea, a "light turnout" means 50,000 sandy, sticky people jammed onto a strand no larger than three football fields (about 1.3 acres); on a "really crowded" day the beach lures 200,000 people. By weight, half of each of these beachgoers is water. Water is a great attractor of its own kind. It streams downhill, as far as it can go, down to the sea: the great mother, drawing her children – droplets of water robed in human flesh – into a thalassic embrace.

4) A rising summer sun slants through a thicket of jewelweed. The heat of the morning, after a cool night, has generated ground-level mist. The undersurface of each leaf wears a glittering bracelet, water beads arranged tastefully along the edge. Each droplet is attached not by glue but by surface tension, the attraction of water molecules to each other. It is a force great enough to overcome gravity.

5) Water hides in hot, supersaturated air, lurking in plain sight to mug the unsuspecting traveler. Like the weight of iron manacles, humidity drags on each step. Liquidity exaggerates the solidity of existence.

6) After a rain shower, a downed moth wheels dizzily on my driveway, its wings so wet that they stick together. Though not much more than a film of water, the weight is sufficient that its wings will not operate. The moth might as well be at the bottom of the sea. With a small plastic plant marker, I lift the moth onto the dry floor of the garage. In time, its burden will lighten.

7) Is there any sound so universally recognizable as that of rain? Rainsound is not rain alone, but water colliding with the mass of earth. At the moment of impact, the kinetic energy of the raindrop dissipates, creating sound waves. The size and speed of the raindrop determines its force of impact. Each variety of rain – drizzle, shower, downpour – has a characteristic distribution pattern of raindrops and therefore a distinct sound. Different surfaces absorb and reflect sound differently: rain patters on leaves, tattoos on dry ground, splats into puddles. And every place is unique – with distinct patterns of vegetation, structures, and substrates. As on a phonograph record, bumps and grooves are the language of sound. Rain, like the needle, translates the physical place into music.

8) Just two summers ago we were enduring a multiyear drought. Days and nights passed without rain. Wells went dry; soil blew away; crisp leaves rained down in a cruel imitation of the real thing. One day at long last, rain came: a deluge of big fat drops that bounced off the parched earth. From the porch, I looked out through the curtain of water. A huge American toad sat in the middle of the front walkway, letting the rain cascade over its back. Toads, like some opera stars, possess heavenly voices that transcend their stout earth-bound figures. As we listened, glorious rainsong washed over us.

9) Late afternoon on a sultry summer day. The sun outlines a web suspended between a porch column and a tall goldenrod. Sitting in the center is a spined micrathena, one of our most common woodland spiders. Abruptly the wind shifts, swirls. A blanket of dark gray clouds smothers the sun. Yet the spider is unmoving. Perhaps her abdominal spines grant her a sense of immunity to danger. Now a fierce wind slings arrows of rain. The web is buffeted by blows from above, below and sideways. The spider bounces up and down in her rigging. Within minutes, the web has been torn to shreds – but the spider has grasped her lifeline, a thick thread diagonally strung from the porch column, and she is hanging on, swinging in the rain. After the storm subsides, she is nowhere to be seen. Has she over-estimated her ability to withstand the onslaught of wind-driven rain? The next morning, not one but two spined micrathenas have woven webs in this spot. The weight of water is only half that of spit and courage.

10) A hickory tree branch overhangs the driveway. Last winter, I could reach the bare gray branch only by leaping up to grab it and bend it down toward me. Now, at midsummer, the branch droops to waist level. Green

sapwood, tender rusty twigs, and broad fragrant leaflets radiating from nut-crowned hubs pull down the branch like a counterbalance on a scale. Where has all this new mass come from? From water: dissolving nutrients in air and soil, then ferrying them through a network of saplines throughout the tree; and from water, reacting with sunlight, chlorophyll and carbon dioxide to form carbohydrates that become living tree tissue. Water constructs a scale with which to weigh itself.

The Larva Ascending

It had all the earmarks of an after-school bullying session. Maybe you've been there; maybe you've even been the one in the middle, surrounded by the ring of tormentors, the different one, alone.

On the surface of a small tree-shaded stream, water striders were flashing back and forth. Not, as I usually see these aquatic insects, skimming over quiet pools with smooth swift strokes. These – perhaps ten of them – had formed a loose circle around something, and they were agitated, leaping into the middle of the circle and leaping back. Standing on the high bank above, I trained my binoculars on the object in the center.

No wonder they were frantic. What was it? It looked like a Loch Ness monster, albeit a one-inch high monster. It loomed over the water striders, a reddish, periscope-shaped *Thing* sticking straight out of the water. One of them would strike at it, it would lurch away; when the circle re-formed, another would hurtle toward it from a different direction. The Thing didn't seem to be a fish, a turtle, or a snake: it didn't extend below the surface.

The water striders accelerated their movements. The Thing turned this way and that, facing the direction of its last harasser. The insects seemed to jump just in front of the Thing. Then abruptly one leaped closer, almost on top of it. The Thing shot straight up in the air a couple of inches and *there it stopped.*

It hung in mid-air, and then it bent in the middle, straightened out, and rose higher.

So, the Thing was a looper. An inchworm, a spanworm, or a cankerworm – a member of the family Geometridae, larvae of small brown moths. These soft-bodied multi-segmented caterpillars lack prolegs in the center of their bodies, so instead of crawling they move by looping: lifting up the abdomen and bringing the rear end close to the front.

This one was, however, dangling over the water, suspended from a branch by a silken thread – a thread it had spun from spinnerets near its mouth, manufacturing its own line as it rappelled down from the tree branch. Up in the forest canopy, it had been spending its first month alive gorging on leaves – even spinning short webs and hitching rides on high breezes to graze from tree to tree.

There were two possible explanations for its current predicament. The silk line could have been an escape thread that it had employed to drop away from a predator, although the strand's length suggested otherwise. More likely the caterpillar was ready to pupate, so it had lowered itself Earthward, where it could find shelter, spin a cocoon, and wait until autumn to emerge as a moth and mate. In either case, its landing in the stream must have been the result of a gross miscalculation, or a gust of wind.

I craned my neck up, up, up. The tree branch was dauntingly high – 25 feet above the stream, higher than a two-story building. Down at the bottom of the thread, there was sudden motion. The caterpillar had begun climbing back the way it had come. It had to loop its rear-most third up to the point where the line ran out from its spinneret, grab the thread, and straighten out its front third, letting the free end of the line collect in wisps around its body. With no leverage, it was hauling itself up by sheer force of will. Against the pull of gravity, open to the wind, exposed to predators. Songbirds, for whom June is peak brood-feeding time, would be only too happy to snatch a fat juicy caterpillar out of thin air.

There was no alternative, though. The water striders were still restless; two got into a tussle, thrashing about until they sprang apart, dripping wet, circling each other like young gunslingers spoiling for a fight. Down was not an option. It was up or out. So the looper continued up.

Up, a half-inch at a time – half of its body length with each loop. The name Geometridae means "Earth-measurers." This one was measuring the distance between survival and oblivion. Twenty-five feet, 12 inches in a foot, altogether about 300 inches. Up, up, no stopping. No snacking. No pausing for breath either – but in fact, the caterpillar was breathing: like an accordion, its segments expelled and ingested air each time it contracted and lengthened. Out, in, out, in: another ten seconds, another inch higher.

After five minutes had passed, the caterpillar had risen above the stream bank; another five minutes and it was level with my eyes. Now a low tree branch was blocking my view; I moved to a new spot. Replacing my binoculars, I couldn't find the caterpillar. I scanned the space where I had last seen it, focusing and refocusing to no avail, as if the air had swallowed it up. Had it fallen? Finally I caught the right angle; it came into view, still curling and stretching. A wriggling, shimmying apparition, it would have been invisible if I hadn't been looking for it.

Up and up and up, it continued. My arms and shoulders were aching, and my neck stiff. A half hour of looping, straight up, with no break – how does that compare with my holding my binoculars in a fixed position over my head? I was discomfited to feel – only – uncomfortable.

Loop and straighten, up and up, into the green. Now only a few inches separated it from the branch that held its thread. The caterpillar bent into a J and twisted its lower body onto a dangling leaf. Suddenly there came a puff of wind – the caterpillar swayed like a trapeze artist from the swinging leaf. It held on, thrust its upper body over the edge, and straightened. And continued looping, across the leaf, up the leaf stem, onto the tree branch.

Its journey had taken nearly an hour. For a month-old caterpillar, an hour is the equivalent of almost four weeks out of my own life.

With no change in the rhythm of loop by loop by loop, it continued along the branch. It was heading toward the thicker part of the branch – the part closer to the tree trunk, closer to land, and closer to another shot at dropping down a thread to reach the Earth.

A dark curtain of leaves now obscured the looper; I had no chance of following it any further. Relieved, I lowered my aching arms. Somewhere, a tiny red caterpillar was pushing on, alone, propelled by will – a force as strong as a silken thread spun in the air.

Who Would Have Thought?

Nature, doing just as we expect, comforts us with a sense of the fundamental order of things: the cycle of seasons, the beauty of a familiar place.

Butterflies float through meadows of summer wildflowers, pausing here and there to sip nectar from the blossoms. Tree leaves turn orange in autumn and fall to the ground, where they dry, fade to brown and become new soil.

Nature, confounding our expectations, surprises us into delight born of insight into the possibilities of the unthought-of.

In the woods, one warm sunny day in late winter or early spring, a dead brown leaf detaches itself from a log, stretches, and floats up to a tree branch, whereupon it turns brilliant orange splattered with black.

The Question Mark butterfly is so called because of the silvery squiggle that adorns the underside of its gaily patterned orange and black wings. But this butterfly is aptly named for another reason: it makes us question our assumptions.

Almost all butterflies in our region pass the winter in an immature form – an egg, a caterpillar or a pupa – waiting for a spring metamorphosis. The Question Mark is one of the very few (the Mourning Cloak and Eastern Comma are others) that overwinters as an adult. It hibernates, hidden behind a loose shred of bark or tucked inside a hollow log, its wings folded. In contrast to the brightly colored topside, the underside of the Question

Mark's wings are dull brown with vein-like lines, and the edges are deeply hooked and lobed: camouflage that enables it to hide in plain sight, like a dead leaf in the detritus of the forest floor.

With the arrival of warmer weather the drowsing Question Mark awakens and emerges from hiding to find a mate. It is one of the earliest, and most brightly colored, harbingers of spring in the woods, still bare of green leaves. The males perch on branches, wings spread in the bright light, while females roam the forest apprising each potential suitor.

Like the wood thrush, or the millipede, the Question Mark is a creature of woodlands, adapted to thrive in the complex web of relationships that comprise the forest. Instead of feeding on nectar from flowers, as do many other butterflies, it seeks out sap from maple, beech or birch trees. Sap flows freely on warm days that follow cold nights; the butterfly takes advantage of the feeding holes tapped by other insects or by the yellow-bellied sapsucker, alighting on tree trunks and folding its wings to pretend to be a leaf as it drinks, hidden from predators.

Or it forages for nutrients from the leavings of other woodland residents: scat, carrion, rotting fruit. The gentle flutter of orange as the butterfly slowly moves its wings, savoring its meal of warm dung freshly laid on the forest floor, beckons us to bend and admire it as we walk through an early summer woods. Can we help but recoil as we approach? Do we not wish instead to find this fragile beauty on a lovely blossom?

If nature were only what we wished for, would we love it so?

Into the Damp

Some days I envy the woodland salamander. Those are the days when the idea of crawling under a cool damp rock, away from the heat and oppression of daily life, seems like an attractive option.

Down there, under the rock − or the matted leaves, the rotting log, the discarded cardboard box − , you stretch out in the darkness, stubby limbs and long tail splayed across your portion of the Earth. The wet air is heavy, but comforting; the fragrance at once mineral-flinty and soil-sweet. Eyes closed, you float, as on a cloud of memory; time slows, now stops. It is now as it was 160 million years ago.

Back then you lived all your days and nights in shallow streams. You had no need for lungs; water provided the oxygen you needed. Land was of use to you only as the container for life-sustaining water.

Then the waters receded. By choice or necessity, you ventured out on land. No water here to swim through, eel-like, but you propelled yourself by wriggling back and forth the way you always had, now gripping the strange solid surface with your new little legs.

Like immigrants everywhere, you clung to some of the old ways even as you embraced the new. You wanted water. You found it lurking under cover, in darkness, saturating the air.

Many of your fellow adventurers gave up on water, developed lungs for breathing, and forgot where they came from. Not you. You relied on your skin, and the way it made intimate contact with the water. You breathed the way you always had: absorbing oxygen and exuding carbon dioxide through your skin, a semi-permeable membrane only a few cells thick. A film of moisture shepherded the diffusing ions back and forth, from air to epithelial cells to blood and back again. You carried that film of water around with you: a reminder not just of your old home, but of what you had been.

And still were. Without water, you'd die. With your thin, scale-less covering, you lost water to evaporation almost as fast as you absorbed it. But as long as you stayed under cover, out of the harsh sun, you were safe.

The cloud of memory dissolves. Here you are, today, just as your ancestors were. The world has warmed and cooled again and again; continents have drifted apart, collided, and separated. The moss-covered red sandstone rock that shelters you was broken off from a ridge, buried in sediment, and heaved up to the surface.

All around you has changed. But you haven't. By all rights, you should have given up long ago.

But then, so should have the Irish monks, safe within their moss-covered stone towers, as civilization collapsed around them, knowledge withered, and darkness descended. Hidden, but not hopeless, they carried the known world into their rock-solid fortresses, and there it lived on. Painstakingly, untiringly, they copied the texts that recorded a culture's wisdom; each generation passed the light of ancient days down to the next, and the next, until the world had come to its senses, reborn anew.

Lately we've seen unprecedented rainfall, flooding, and humidity. Water is returning. Land is receding.

Is this what you've been waiting for, under your rock?

Fall

Here's Looking at You

Returning to the Central Bucks area after a long "sabbatical" in the southeastern Tennessee mountains, I feel as if I've taken off my glasses and have to re-focus. I'm still blinking.

The southern Appalachians are a Times Square of nature. On every forest hike I'd find myself thinking: now this is how a woods should look and sound. Green leaves of all shapes and sizes hang like banners from understory to tree canopy; wildflowers cover every available space like the remains of a ticker-tape parade; curled lichens sheathe tree trunks like so many tattered theater flyers tacked to lightpoles. Spiders, millipedes, snails, beetles, and snakes throng the trails; birds sing and swoop through the air; streams brim with fish, mollusks, and crustaceans. Hidden caves and grottoes shelter odd creatures and rare plants. From a clifftop perch, the sprawling panorama unfolds as dramatically as the view from the tallest skyscraper.

What is writ large in those mountains seems jotted on a grain of rice here. The reasons for the remarkable biodiversity of the Tennessee mountains are as various as the forms of life that inhabit the area, but chiefly it is the lack of development (albeit with much of the forestland used for logging), which has left plenty of space for plants and animals to thrive. Open space in Central Bucks inspires fierce protection battles, but the space is open only between huge swaths of land that's inhospitable to most life other than the two-legged variety. There is green here, yet much of the green is an illusion: a lawn desert where nothing but grass lives, or woods that are like old-age homes for trees because deer are consuming the younger generation.

And yet, flourishing here – even in cramped yards in the center of historic Doylestown, where I live now – is one of the most beguiling of nature's forms. It's right beneath our feet, and it's all over. It lives in decaying wood and bark, so it's common in forest debris, but it's just as comfortable in wood-chip mulch.

You may have to squint, but you'll know it when you see it: Clusters of tiny wooly tan goblets, no more than a quarter-inch in diameter. They start out with closed, sunken tops, looking like miniature knitted winter hats. The cups eventually open to reveal a clutch of glossy black bits, flattened and triangular in profile, like lentils or minuscule ikebana stones. Each of these sixteenth-inch diameter peridioles is attached to the inside wall of the cup with a slender coiled filament. These structures look like eggs, and in fact perform a similar reproductive function; they're spore cases.

Eggs in a cup: No wonder Cyathus striatus is commonly called a "birds-nest fungus." Even to the naked eye the structure is fascinating; under a magnifying lens it's downright deceiving. Like the avian nest, the fungal nest holds offspring until the moment is right for them to leave and start a new life on their own. But whereas juvenile birds are nudged out of the nest by their parents as soon as they can fly, in the case of the mushroom the send-off is actually built into the structure. How? Hint: these fungi are also called "splash cups."

There's a white picket fence around the border of my house. The fence encloses a line of hedges tucked into bed with hardwood mulch, and on the mulch happily grow colonies of Cyathus. The lower half of each picket is dotted with small black circles. To the casual observer they look like mud splashes, spattered there when the rain hits the mulch.

They're splashes, all right. But the dots are not mud. They're the spore cases of the birds-nest fungus. The inner wall of each "nest" slants out at the precise angle that will eject the spore case when a raindrop hits the cup. The "egg" is expelled upward by the force of the water, up to a yard or more away, where it sticks to the closest surface. The dots are obvious on a white fence or siding, but if you examine the underside of nearby leaves, or the soil surrounding the mushrooms, you'll see the eggs there also. Once stuck to a surface, the spore cases are ready to germinate, although they'll do nothing unless the substrate is dead wood.

Shortly after I'd settled in to my new home, the balmy Indian summer abruptly gave way to autumn chill. Overnight, windy rains sloshed the eggs out of the birds-nests. OK, so there's no Times Square here. No ticker tape parades for my return, either. Just an exuberant toast from nature's bottomless cup. To life!

Salute the Colors

What's your favorite three-color-combination? Red white and blue, maybe, like the U.S. flag? or perhaps black, white and red: a hot fudge sundae?

This was one of the out-of-left-field questions posed by my son's teacher on a back-to-school survey this year. The questionnaire was ingeniously designed not only to shake and wake the students out of their summer lethargy, but also to help the teacher get to know a whole new crop of kids all at once – while also giving the students an inkling of the teacher's own personality.

Now, that question got me to thinking about what nature's favorite three-color combination might be. How could you define "favorite," anyway? The most common, I guess. That could be brown, green and blue: the colors of a tree against the sky. Or blue, green, and white: waves on a windswept sea. Common? You want common? How about brown, black, and beige: ants excavating an anthill, underfoot, everywhere you look. And don't forget about winter whites: white-gray and white-blue and white-white: snow, falling, blowing and drifting under a faraway sun.

But maybe "favorite" isn't the most prevalent combination. Maybe instead it's the most brilliant, blazing, unforgettable one: the yellow, red, and orange of sugar maples in autumn. Or the black, orange, and blue of the monarch butterfly flitting overhead in a cloudless summer sky. Or even gold, green, and silver: pinwheel mushrooms, rimmed with mist, materializing in the grass after a rain.

Maybe "favorite" is the color of things that are hidden away and hard to find. The turquoise, silver and blue of a glacial lake high in the mountains. The scarlet, black and green of a tanager perched deep in the woods; the black, red and brown of a salamander sheltering under a fallen leaf; the bruise-red, new-apple green and paper-bag brown of a wild ginger flower resting on the ground, tucked under the canopy of its own leaf.

Favorite – perhaps precious because it doesn't last. Like the blue-black, silvery purple, pearly white of seashells bathed in seawater, which by the time you get them home turn dull and unremarkable. Or maybe *favorite* because it's what will be the same for your descendant's descendants as it is for you, like the green, gray and black of lichens on a granite boulder. Or the color of things that go by so fast you almost miss them, like the red, black, green of a hummingbird pausing to sip nectar from a cardinal flower. Or the ones you don't see unless you get down on your hands and knees, like emerald-green, nut-brown and crimson-red: a collage of moss, bark sliver, and spider mite. Or the ones meant not to be seen: algae-green, mud-brown, sunlight-yellow: a pair of frog's eyes just sticking up above the pond surface.

Colors you can hold and feel: black, red, green – a firefly. Colors that are always just ahead out of reach: creamy white, caramel tan and chocolate brown – sea foam blown across a beach by rising winds. Colors you daren't hold that are borne on their own wind: the black, yellow and orange of a hornet. Colors you can taste, like the red, green and brown of a wild strawberry picked in a muddy meadow, flavors of sun, grass and earth.

Colors you can see after the sun goes down. Black, white, red: stars and planets speckling the night sky. Colors you can hear after the sun goes down. Black, white, red: a lake-calling loon.

School is one set of questions after another, years of them, then you're out of school and you need to make the questions up yourself. Asking the right ones makes all the difference.

Slow Motion

In a world where it's hard to find the time to stop and smell the roses, once in a while it's enough just to slow down. Take a ride down Gayman Road in Plumstead Township, a mile-long ribbon of narrow rural blacktop that is surrounded for most of its length by the Gaymans' farm, much of which has been preserved with county and municipal funds. A year or so ago the speed limit was lowered to 25 mph – a pace usually saved for congested neighborhoods or commercial districts – to discourage the use of the road as a shortcut during rush hour.

I don't know why anyone would choose this road as a shortcut. Besides being narrow, jouncy, high-crowned, ditch-lined and steep, it takes a jog over a one-lane S-bridge. The speed limit is the maximum safely attainable over much of the route anyway. One might as well slow down and take in the view.

At speed, everything blurs together and becomes a continuous undifferentiated scene. At a full stop, what one notices are the details. Slow motion facilitates a continuously shifting point of view that allows one to subconsciously assemble the details into patterns.

The road links two ridgetops, with the bridge crossing at the lowest point, where the North Branch of the Neshaminy Creek meanders. The Gayman farm spreads across the valley and up the hills on both sides, covering several hundred acres.

The view into the valley is typical Pennsylvania unspectacular. Compared with the vast expanses of Heartland cornfields that stretch from horizon to horizon, the Gayman farm is downright tiny. Compared with New England's rocky mountainsides, to which farms cling tenaciously like goats, the rolling hills that make up the Gayman farm could be called flat. Compared with the thousands of head of cattle that roam the ranges in the

Great Plains, the Gayman herd of beef cows is about as impressive as a glass of water is to the ocean.

Nonetheless I always find that at the crest of the hill, as I start to descend, it is as if the car loses its will to go. The hill steepens but the car slows. It's like those magnetic hills in weird out-of-the-way places, where you drive your car forward but it looks like you're going backwards. As the road dips and the horizon rises, there is a point where the view, a half-mile in any direction, is entirely of cultivated lands (along with an occasional house or silo), stretching across the valley to the other side. Invariably there will be cows standing impassively by the fence, or sitting in the shade, chewing; calves nuzzling their mother as she swats flies with her tail. It's a scene that could have existed hundreds of years ago.

At the bottom of the hill is the S-bridge. Look closely at its fieldstone supports and you see the datestone – 1887 – and the name, Gayman's Ford bridge. The Gaymans have been here since before there was a bridge. When Christian Gayman settled here, in 1855, the pace was slower, the roads mere dirt tracks; whether a creek could be forded easily depended on the season.

Cross the bridge and the land rises again. The valley is shorn of trees. It is like a bowl that reflects the unbroken sky above. Here, space expands as time slows. One senses the terrain, the rhythms of ridge and valley and stream. The checkerboard of planted fields covers the rolling landscape like a blanket laid atop a sleeping child. Lines of soybeans, laid out as with a straight-edge, seem to fan out as you go by, the lines converging on a constantly moving point.

This is what biologist Renè Dubos called a "humanized landscape." Many people enjoy viewing wild places from outside, or even being in a wilderness for short periods of time; but humans are not, for the most part, comfortable living in wilderness. We modify the landscape to suit our purposes. That the modifications have unintended consequences which adversely affect our environment is an issue we have only recently been forced to address, as the seriousness of the consequences becomes clear. But, as Dubos pointed out, the modifications we make to the landscape imbue it with cultural and emotional qualities.

No, the Gayman Road landscape is not wilderness. It is land managed for a human purpose. It is managed as part of a continuity in time. There is a past existent here, and there is a future inherent within in it. Perhaps that is why it is conducive to contemplation. The word contemplate derives from the Latin words for "in the templum." Templum – from which we derive "temple" – means "the place for observing things to come."

When I am here, I feel connected to the world of the past and the world to come. The power of this place is that it creates a connection that transforms me from observer into participant.

Whether what we do with the land we occupy creates a lasting place or a passing scene depends on how well we love it. Here, on Gayman Road, is a place. It is worth slowing down for.

El Dorado

You move out to the country and they put up a city right in your backyard.

The foundation is in the ground by spring. Sometimes it's a tear-down job and they use last year's foundation, build right on top of it. Other times it's brand new; it just sprouts up. In either case they put on one monotonous layer after another for months on end. They don't use a crane: they operate from the inside out. There's the core with all the essential services, including the circulation system to move things up and down. Cantilevered out from that in whorls, floor after floor after floor of them, are the balconies. That's where they catch some rays in their spare hours.

It's insidious, that's what. At first you don't even notice; it's all kind of background scenery. But it creeps up on you until suddenly one day in late summer you turn around and there's a whole cluster of them. Looming, blocking your view. The top is so gaudy, so "look-at-me," it's embarrassing. Row upon row of tiny yellow baubles, arching over each other. When you get up close you can smell the air freshener.

Of course with that kind of tawdry spectacle you can expect the wrong kind of crowd to start coming. The kind that wears outfits with horizontal stripes, and loves to stick its nose into anybody's business. There's never just one of them. First one bumbles in, then another shows up, then another and then the whole place is covered with them. Very fickle, they are: as soon as the good stuff is gone, they move on. But the proprietor refills the stock overnight so wouldn't you know it, next morning there they are again, ready for action.

That's life in Goldenrod City. Its architecture is ancient, but George Jetson would feel right at home here, surrounded by weirdly shaped structures and amidst a constant hum of flying objects. Tall straight spires are capped with dreadlocks of tiny yellow flowers. Buzzing here, there and everywhere are, not personal copters, but winged insects on the prowl for food. On a sunny day with the flowers at their peak of bloom the plumes are fast-food meccas crawling with bees, beetles and flies, all of whom are gathering pollen and slurping nectar from the drive-through blossom bar.

Such frenetic activity is bound to attract the attention of those ladies of leisure, the crab spiders. These grande dames can't even be bothered to spin a web. They sit motionless hidden in a flowerhead; camouflaged by their pale colors and drab lines. Eventually some unsuspecting member of the insect working class will come along. Poor victim, enticed by the flower's heady perfume, mesmerized by the blaring come-hither yellow, and focused on the task of getting a meal for the family – bloop! Pincers strike, mouthparts bite, and you can put a *finis* to that life story.

Every city has its squatters. In Goldenrod City they start young, even before they can crawl. Mother gall fly drops off a clutch of eggs, and the hatchlings set up housekeeping just as if they had paid the rent. The little squirmers even bring their own paint, which they apply liberally to the stem walls. Instant remodeling: enzymes in the coating cause the walls to expand. Pretty soon it starts to look like the Space Needle, with a bulbous protrusion in the upper floors. The interlopers spend the winter eating themselves out of house and home. Literally. They eat the inside of their new house. Well, easy come, easy go. When spring rolls around, they decide to join the ranks of responsible creatures, so they put on wings and fly off without bothering to fix the mess they've made. They're not called gall flies for nothing.

Not that it's life on easy street here. Those gall bulbs make obvious targets for those in the know. So anyone – anyone who's a parasitoid wasp – can drill down to the master bedroom, drop off an egg and not give it a second thought. The wasp youngster wakes up next to his own private pantry: a side of fly larva. Fat and happy by spring, he takes off the way he got in, out the back door.

Then there's the capo di capo of the neighborhood, the downy woodpecker. Only the best, biggest galls for this bird; the biggest, juiciest fly larvae. Rat-a-tat-tat: "Come on, I know you're in there." Can't run, can't hide. The jackhammer doesn't miss.

Postcard from Goldenrod City: You want rural serenity? Pave it over.

Book of Revelations

Autumn leaves speak to us of things unseen. The messages are written, not in ink as they are on the literal leaves of a book, but in the ancient elements of fire and air, earth and water.

We are taught never to look at the sun. In the fall, we can see the sun without looking at it. Turning leaves appropriate the sun's palette to paint for us the flames we cannot see directly. The sun's rays stoke the leafy fire; leaves that catch the strongest light burn the most brilliant red and gold. Wind fans the blaze; it leaps and flares.

A breeze, blue sky, a bench: no more perfect combination exists in this season. I lie back and gaze straight up. Oak, hickory, ash and tulip trees form an airy canopy overhead. They bend and sway. The leaves shiver.

One detaches itself. It does not merely fall: it glides, twirls, slides, pirouettes. It catches the wind I cannot see, riding it up and down with the powerful grace of a surfer. Another one hangs in the air, held motionless by an invisible updraft. A troop of leaflets dive from a branch all at once; their parachutes catch and hold; they drift slowly down. A flat leaf skims sideways, does a loop-de-loop and rights itself, like a toy balsa wood plane.

As leaves fall, they reveal hidden worlds in the trees. Here, all spring and summer, families were born and raised, behind a curtain of greenery. Nests are tucked in niches and wedged into crooks: a neat round robin's nest, lined with smoothed mud, not a stick out of place; the squirrels' abode, like a messy teenager's room, with leaves and twigs poking out at crazy angles; a pendulous paper wasp nest made of overlapping scales, hanging like a lantern.

On the ground, leaves amplify the tread of the unseen. A steady rhythmic rustling in the brush turns out to be a flock of newly arrived migrating white-throated sparrows scratching for seeds with their feet. A staccato hop, hop then a scramble, is the squirrel; a whisper could be a snake or a fast-moving vole. After dark, raccoons, possums, cats and other creatures of the night, give away their cover with the rasp and crunch that accompanies each footfall.

With a super-sensitive microphone, you could hear the disappearance of leaves. Earthworms slip out of their burrows at night and munch on them, as do mites, pillbugs, and millipedes. Most of the work, though, is done in silence. Cool autumn nights wring moisture out of the air; dew settles on the leaves. Moisture creates ideal conditions for bacteria and fungi to thrive, and leaves are their meal. The sweet tang of an autumn morning is the fragrance of their feast. It is the aroma of creation, the beginning of earth.

Leaves disappear, but they are not gone. The minerals they are composed of, and the energy they contain in the form of sugars, are transformed into soil, that thin layer between air and rock on which life depends. Soil nurtures the seeds that grow into trees that make the leaves that fall to the ground and start again – a never-ending story.

A burning leaf pile is a sad sight: fire makes heat out of the leaves' energy and smoke out of the minerals, all of which dissipates up into the air. It is a short story with an abrupt ending. The much wiser practice is to chop, mulch and compost those surplus leaves. On their own, leaves will eventually make their own fire – the fire of the sun.

Smooth or Chunky?

Now which way? I've reached the end of the woods trail; to return to the car, I can either walk the paved road that angles around the frozen hayfield, or cut through the lumpy, muddy field. No contest. I take the shortcut, across the tussocky residue of last season's crop.

What appeals me to me about this course is not just that it's a shortcut. It's that it requires effort. And that means it's not mind-numbing. Walking on uneven ground requires you to pay attention to the feel of the terrain and to anticipate obstacles ahead. One doesn't stride across the field; one tramps, up and over the mounded earth, bobbing on the shallow waves, making the walk a series of tiny challenges to balance and agility; each step provides a bit of information about the earth beneath one's feet. By the time I get to the parking lot I'm invigorated by the journey; if I'd gone the other way, I'd have been fixated on the end of the road.

For me, the road not taken is the preferable choice. Give me the soft ground next to the sidewalk, the trail made of mossy tree roots grasping a rocky slope. I'll sacrifice a quaint wooden footbridge in favor of hopping across stones in the creek.

Decades ago, researchers confirmed what nurses and waitresses have always known: walking on flat surfaces makes the feet sore and legs tired. We weren't meant to have a challenge-free life. People, it turns out, feel better walking and standing on rough uneven surfaces than they do on flat smooth floors and walkways. Unevenness stimulates blood vessel growth. It also strengthens foot muscles that assist in stability.

Indeed, according to a recent study, a rubber mat that simulates cobblestones provides equivalent benefits. Of course, where science runs, commerce follows. You can now buy bumpy mats to imitate nature's path if you can't find the real thing to walk on. Want something more portable? There's a new shoe design that puts the uneven surface under your feet wherever you go.

Although a woodland is my favorite place to walk, I regularly join the human hamsters on a treadmill in the Y, staring out the wall of windows at what passes for a view – the lawn. The bleak autumn landscape is enlivened by the spectacle of leaves, blown from the oak trees bordering the site, skittering across the ground and landing in apparently random clumps. After a recent snowstorm, clusters of brown leaves resting on the surface gave the whitened lawn a brindle coat. Because dark colors absorb the sun's warmth while light colors reflect it, the snow melted much faster around the leaves. The mottled surface gave rise to invisible currents of air as sunlight heated the dark leaves and the ground under them; the warm air rose, cooled and sank back.

The movement of air over the unevenly warmed lawn is in microcosm the same process of differential heating by which all surface winds develop. Winds arise from contrasts in color (dark vs. light), topography (mountain vs. valley), or material (water vs. land). The movement of air around the globe, and variations and contrasts between air masses, create our changeable weather. If the Earth were a smooth, uncluttered billiard ball instead of a rough-textured multicolored ragdoll head, life would be much less interesting.

Unevenness is what led to the creation of our planet in the first place. When the cosmos was forming, the fog of energy that turned into matter did so unevenly; areas with different densities acted like cosmic seeds, rather like airborne dust particles that attract cloud-borne water vapor and so form raindrops. These clumps of matter became galaxies, stars and planets.

No, I'd rather not smooth the course. It's unevenness that forces adaptation, roughness that stimulates creativity and resilience, variation that channels energy. On the PBJ of life, I'll take chunky.

Warm Fuzzies

Bears stare at me from every room of my house. Furry, cuddly, perpetually ready with a sympathetic ear, they and others of their kind – the stuffed set – satisfy an atavistic human longing, even for those of us with living, breathing pets. Somewhere deeply embedded in our psyche, formed in the early days of our species, there must be a collective memory of warm fuzzy companions shepherding us through the cold darkness. That would explain the partiality that most people display for wildlife that resembles the ur-teddy.

It's on a rainswept fall day that such wuzzly comfort seems most enticing. Raw, damp chilly air has barged in, dispossessing Indian summer like an uninvited guest throwing open the front door and settling in on the sofa. Overnight, a brutish wind has stripped the trees of their finery and strewn leaves in the ground. By morning the leaves give off an indescribable fragrance – sweet and spicy, tangy and rich, like frolicsome summer fermenting into a tea of winter fortitude.

Wet leaves render driving hazardous and train rides a mess of delays. Travel is treacherous at this time of year for woolly bears too. The fuzzy red-and-brown-banded caterpillars, larvae of the tiger moth (Pyrrharctia isabella), are on the move in September and October, hunting for a site in a rock crevice or under a piece of bark where they will overwinter before emerging in spring to pupate. They seek shelter not only to hide from predators, particularly skunks, but also to protect themselves from the coming cold. For that reason they are often found where sun-warmed spots are likely to be: along edges and openings, on roads and walkways. While they can move fast for a caterpillar – up to four feet a minute – woolly bears are not always speedy enough to avoid being smashed into roadkill or even sidewalkkill and trailkill. But perhaps there are not as many victims as there would be if the caterpillars weren't so goshdarn cute and pick-up-able.

On this gray day, I spot a woolly bear on a flat rock near the house, not moving anyplace in particular. I nudge it onto a leaf, then gently transfer it into one cupped hand. It promptly curls into a spiral. Its "wool" is a soft but stiff bristle, like the mohair of antique teddy bears, not the namby-pamby plush of modern-day ones. It's so light it is only barely present. One can't hold it too loosely or it will blow away, nor too tightly or it will be crushed. I make my hands a globe, securing it, and blow gently on it, as if warming a glowing ember. It is the color and weight of a dry leaf; indeed both of them approach a winter of waiting that precedes a springtime transformation – the leaf will begin to turn into soil, the caterpillar will become a moth. I hold it close, as if by so doing, I can stave off its future life as a wholly different creature. The woolly bear remains curled up, protecting itself from danger. (Me!)

Nature is profoundly indifferent to our affections. A few weeks ago, a long-horned beetle somehow found its way into the space between the window and the screen, and couldn't find its way back out. Usually I can trap such blunderers with a plastic cup and a card, and carry them to safety. This beetle, though, refused to capitulate to the cup. It squiggled out, releasing an odor that may have been intended to gag me (me!) but instead made me smile, because it smelled like bananas. The beetle then relocated to the very top of the window where I couldn't reach it. Over the next few days I raced over with the cup whenever it ventured partway down, but each time it escaped. After a week, it finally did go all the way to the bottom sill, but by then it had expired. Preferring independence to being transported against its will, it died with dignity.

Reaching out to other species is, more often than not, a one-way affair. The hours I spend disentangling Japanese honeysuckle runners from young trees in the woods are rewarded with silence from the saplings, or, worse, sneak attacks from raspberry thorns hiding amongst the dense vines. Even the sharp prick of the thorn cannot compare to the pain in my heart that I feel when, having just refilled the birdfeeders, a chickadee gives out its alarm call branding me (me!) as a potential predator.

But if we give our fellow species a place to live they will return the favor, even if that is not the purpose of what they offer. Instead of the positive reinforcement that I would prefer, I take comfort in those moments, these gifts to the senses that impart knowledge of the physical world. Like the bewitching scent of wet leaves, an accidental gift from the trees produced by life-sustaining decay; the fruit-fragranced determination of a stubborn, doomed beetle; the ethereal brush of the wooly bear against my skin as it rolls up in self-defense. Moments in which my pleasure is produced by death-defying nature. This is cold comfort, not the warm fuzzy embrace of a favorite stuffed animal. I wrap it around myself like a coat borne against the chill.

Now Playing

Crisp days framed with soft golden light usher in the new fall season. It's a good time to take in a show at the County Theater. The non-profit, member-supported Doylestown movie house is renowned for the independent films presented in its art-deco style building. But some of the best performances take place off-screen.

Cue lighting: It's just before dusk. Orange-red light warms the horizon; straight up there's still cool blue light.

Cue sound: staccato bursts of bat-like twittering.

And *action*!

Voices:

Up in the sky, it's a bird, it's a plane, it's –

Auntie Em, Auntie Em! It's a twister! A twister!

They're heeeere…

[Above the theater's chimney, a mass of birds – 50, 75, a hundred – circle: some clockwise, some counterclockwise; then they all organize into a spiraling cohesion with the chimney at the center point. Each small, dark cigar-shaped bird rapidly flaps its pointed wings while simultaneously steering up, down or sideways to avoid crashing into its fellows, the trees or the rooftops. Occasionally one will drop straight down, make a pass at the chimney, and swoop back up into the gyre.]

Narrator:

Every fall, chimney swifts that have spent the summer nesting in the forests and towns of eastern North America begin migrating to their winter habitats in Peru, Chile and Brazil. Swifts are committed aerialists, constantly on the wing: catching insects, courting, mating, never on a perch during the day. They do descend to Earth in order to build their nests in hollow trees and chimneys, the same kinds of places that they favor for overnight roosts.

As the days grow shorter, swifts take off from their breeding territories and head south toward the Gulf Coast: flying, flying, flying, averaging almost 30 miles an hour as they go; flying at times as high as or even higher than the cloud layer; winging down the Atlantic Flyway over the coastal plain, or along the Piedmont valley east of the Appalachian ridge. As night begins to fall, flocks of weary swifts descend from the sky, looking for somewhere to rest.

[Wide shot: The swirling mass forms a conical shape that's broad at the top and narrow at the bottom, tailing over the chimney like a funnel. Zoom in to a close-up shot of one bird: follow it around and around, a dizzying pace. Medium shot: at any random spot in the funnel, individuals race past each other, or break out into twos and threes that streak off at a new angle, but most simply hurtle by. Jump cut to chimney top: the bird at the bottom of the funnel tail hurtles toward the chimney at breakneck speed, wings flapping, then suddenly seems to shudder, crumple its wings, slow to a stop directly above the open shaft and drop straight down, head-first. Immediately, so does the bird right behind it. Then the next and the next.]

Narrator:

As if the film were running backwards, the swifts vanish like liquid smoke pouring into the chimney. Hundreds, even thousands of swifts roost together during migration. Here, feet clinging to the shaft's inner surface, they will sleep, awaiting the dawn. These are the lucky ones; they've found a place to rest before the next leg of their exhausting intercontinental trip. An uncapped chimney is a rarity these days, almost as rare as a big old hollow tree.

Each night the swifts relinquish their home in the sky, but they seem to wait as long as possible – till the last minute of sunlight – flying ever more frantically, faster and faster, squeezing the last moment of whirling, spinning, spiraling movement out of the air itself, pressing it into the chimney, where the flock holds it close between their feathers, holding it till sunrise, which will come, surely.

[Hold shot on the chimney, then pan up slowly to the sky overhead. Empty of birds. Light slowly drains from the clouds. Darkness.]
Roll credits.
Cue applause.

The Power of Place

Power can be an outstretched fist – or an outstretched hand. We're inclined to think of power as something that constrains or even diminishes another. Power can exclude, like the lines on a map that define property: by representing the power to keep out, they draw a community as a collection of places that touch but do not intersect. But there is another kind of power that, when shared, increases the recipient's power without lessening the giver's.

One day in September, 2003, residents of Plumstead Township dedicated a new nature park, named Allohaken. A Lenape word, "allohaken" means "powerful place." It's related to the word for teacher (allohakasin) – that is, one who has power over another.

Dedication day began with a deluge. Rains saturated the grounds the day and night before, and kept coming during the morning. As the start of the ceremony approached, the rain slackened, then retreated, but a phalanx of heavy gray clouds lingered overhead. Instead of rain, though, the afternoon brought a torrent of acknowledgements and thank-you's. Individuals, families, officials, committees and boards accepted congratulations, having worked for years to mark this land off as special –

first by saving it from development as a school, then by establishing it as a nature park.

Chief Robert Red Hawk Ruth of the Lenape Nation told the crowd a story. When William Penn first met our people, said the Chief, he asked, how many are there of you? We had a hard time answering that question, Red Hawk said, because we counted in our family the trees, the birds, the rocks … all the elements of the natural world.

Three Lenape women paced out a sinuous dance. The beads and bells sewn to their clothes clacked and jingled with each bouncing step, sounding like rain blowing through leaves, while Red Hawk sang a song of thanks that we had all reached this day. Brownies and Boy Scouts planted trees. When the Brownies finished, they said to Red Hawk, "Wanishi!" Thank you. The Chief smiled in delight. Wanishi, he said, laughing. To close the ceremony, he chanted a Lenape blessing, honoring the four directions: Grandfather in the North, keeper of rock; Grandfather in the East, wind; Grandmother in the South, fire, and Grandfather in the West, water. The crowd drifted away; the park now officially named.

Allohaken is forty acres, more or less, in the shape of an L. From its eastern border along Landisville Road, the park slopes almost imperceptibly down to the Pine Run creek. Oaks, dogwoods, hickories, viburnums, ashes and spicebush mix in a convivial, alluvial society. On the other side of the creek, woods march a quarter-mile up the hill along Bergstrom Road. There are no trails yet, so from an opening along the road, strike out through the woods, following deer paths and dry streamlet beds, until you get to a tributary of the creek. Look for the hoofprints on the low spots, ford the stream on stepping stones. Across the far bank, the forest canopy gives way suddenly to sunlight and sky. Here, about 400 feet from the road, is an open meadow as wide as the woods are long, bordered by trees and divided by a hedgerow into two rectangles, one twice the size of the other. Deer, voles, foxes, and polecats have the run of the fields; hawks soar on the wind above; sparrows, bluebirds, and jays dart in and out of edge thickets. Cross back into the woods below the meadow, past muddy places where springs bubble up and skunk cabbages flourish. The puddles and trickles meld into tiny channels that join together, winding downhill to the creek. At the bottom of the hill, rock ledges trace an old abandoned roadbed along the main stem of the Pine Run. Follow it back west, back to the modern road. You've gone in four directions, now.

This piece of earth is a remnant of what the township was like at a time when there were far fewer people than trees, and birds, and rocks. The Lenape are a remnant of what they once were, too, a scrap of cloth in a fabric that was torn apart and cast to the winds long ago. We live now in a community of keep-out straight lines. Yet this piece of earth brought us, all of us, together, in struggle and in celebration.

People came together because we agreed on the importance of this place. By agreeing that it is important, we have granted this place power over us. But we are increased, and the place is not diminished; indeed its power grows as we honor it. The straight lines on our maps cannot constrain it, the directions of the compass float above and below it. Trees lie down in the woods, and from their final resting places rise new trees. Birds sing from their branches, and their roots grasp the rocks. Our brothers and sisters surround us.

In this place, we are too many to be counted. As much power as we are willing to grant a place, we will get it back. Sharing power, we create a family.

Fruit on the Floor

Harvest Moon rises perfectly round and plump, glowing amber. It looks close enough to touch. But as soon as you reach for it, it slips out of your grasp, away up into the trees.

There, little moonlets hang. Perfectly round and plump, glowing amber. They look good enough to eat. But pluck one from the branch, bite down: it's lemon-tart, bitter and hard, not sweet.

No these moonlets must set before being eaten.

Lower your gaze and hunch down, among the dried leaves and tufts of grass pocketed with root crevasses. Down here, away from heaven's gaze, lie our native tree-fruits of autumn: crabapple, pawpaw, persimmon. Fallen fruits, whose fall signals that the time is right. Fruit on the floor is the ripest of all.

Crabapples on the tree are greenish-yellow, with the fresh-faced sheen of youth. As they mature they put on a rosy blush and a cloudy matte finish freckled with harmless wax-dwelling fungi. The apples' natural wax coating (it shines when you rub it on your clothes) keeps water from either penetrating or evaporating through the skin, preventing rot while keeping the fruit-juiciness that makes the apple appetizing.

Appetizing, that is, if you like sour apples. Despite its common name, the "sweet crabapple" – the only crabapple native to our area – bears tart, sour fruit. Good for jellies, and for cider, and for tossing across a field, but for not for sweet loveliness.

It is the crabapples imported from Asia and Eurasia that are sweet. Luckily for the forager, the many varieties of crabapples merrily hybridize, natives with imports alike. You never know what you are in for. Maybe the apple you pick up will sit sweetly on your tongue, and maybe not. It's a crab shoot.

You'll find crabapple trees, like most members of the rose family, in sunny spots – roadsides, old field thickets, fencerows. Pawpaws, though, flourish down low, in floodplains where it's cool and moist and shady. Once a pawpaw tree finds a good spot, it seriously settles in, spreading by underground stems to clone itself over and over. A pawpaw patch is a wondrous thing to find, for here the forager will be rewarded with armfuls of exotic fruit.

Tucked under wide, teardrop-shaped leaves as long as a forearm, pawpaw fruits develop into greenish cylinders a few inches long. Hard and yellowish on the small tree, there is no point in plucking them: not till cool autumn nights arrive will the fruits will ripen and fall. As the skin of the fallen fruit sags, darkens, and wrinkles, the inside softens.

Peel off the skin to uncover an orange-yellow, pulpy, spoonable mass. A bit of banana, a bit of apple, a bit of vanilla: the pawpaw fruit seems tropical. Indeed, it is the northern-most member of the custard-apple family.

In the pulp lie a half dozen flattish mahogany seeds in clear membranous sacs. Although opossums, raccoons and squirrels gobble up pawpaws, they leave the seeds where they've found the fruit, which gives the tree no reproductive advantage over its own cloning. Some researchers hypothesize that pawpaws evolved very large fruits and seeds to be eaten by very large mammals, such as the mastodon, which would disperse the seeds in scat. Deprived of the service of these animals, extinct since the last Ice Age, the pawpaw has been left to its own devices.

Persimmons, too, are probably Ice Age relicts, and they too now spread by cloning rather than by seed dispersion. Unlike crabapples and pawpaws, though, which are small, spreading understory trees, the persimmon − a member of the ebony family − shoots up tall and straight. If you spot its distinctive square-fissured bark in autumn, look up into its canopy. There are the bright orange, plum-sized fruits. But the two-toned, tapering persimmon leaves point straight down, as if saying, "Look below!"

Reach up to a low branch and pull off a fruit. It feels good in the hand, soft and edible. Look below! say the leaves. You take a bite. Ohhh. We warned you! say the leaves. The still-hanging persimmon fruit packs a secret weapon. One bite dries your mouth faster than Rosie's quicker-picker-upper. Persimmon is the quicker-puckerer.

But just wait. Wait till the fruit has plopped from the tree onto the forest floor, where it languishes like a half-spent balloon. Grab it, if you can, before the local woodland creatures do. Ripe persimmon has a papaya-like consistency, and a flavor all its own: a bit like pear, a bit like apricot, and much that is unlike anything else.

Fruit on the floor goes against everything they tell you. They tell you to want a clean, shiny, round fruit, easily plucked from its neat pyramidal pile under the bright lights, tasting just like what you expect it to taste like. Fruit on the forest floor is hard to find. And when you do find it, it's mud-spotted, fungi-speckled, fall-dented; misshapen, pockmarked, pitted. You never know if it'll be ripe, and even if it is ripe, every fruit tastes a little different.

Compared with the perfect ideal of the Harvest Moon, fallen fruits fall short. But the moon is perfect in a moonly way. Fall fruits attain perfection not by looking like the moon, full and round and luminous, but by looking like fruit, ripened by the fullness of time.

Leaves, Leaving

The last time I saw my great-Aunt Nett, about 20 years ago, she was standing at her front door with one hand raised in a farewell wave to our departing car. Some months after we parted, she died peacefully in her sleep. Now, the last sight I had of her is the one image that remains eternally fixed in my mind's eye.

In autumn, trees too hold their limbs in a gesture of frozen goodbye, as their falling leaves journey on without them.

Change is the essential condition of experience. So, loss – the loss of the present – is inherent in existing. To cope with loss, humans, blessed (or burdened) with self-awareness, go through a grieving process. The hurt heals, life goes on: we endure.

Built into a tree is the knowledge that change happens. Trees anticipate loss. They know how to shed leaves.

A leaf is the answer to the question, why a tree? Each leaf is an organized collection of green cells; it exists to convert sunlight into sugar. Leaves could do their job flat on the ground in the same manner that lily pads float on a pond, but after covering the available surface, there's nowhere to go but up. By reaching high into the sky, and filling three-dimensional space with branches, a single tree creates homesites for thousands of leaves; then, having staked out its territory, the tree exploits green power to create durable wood tissues that enable leaves to work that space year after year.

Leaves of course don't exist on their own, and green cells don't just sit in isolated splendor within the leaf. Much of the leaf structure is dedicated to integrating the leaf into the whole living tree system: pores support gas exchange; the leaf surface, evaporation of water; veins, the movement of sap. This intricate structure requires energy to maintain, but as long as the leaf is producing an energy surplus, the tree is content to support it. As summer wanes, though, light availability declines, and the leaf becomes more expensive; eventually it costs more than it brings in. The leaf separates from the tree where its stem joins a twig, and the leaf falls.

But the leaf doesn't just fall. Look closely at a twig, especially under the buds, and you'll see small areas that are lighter or darker, or smoother or rougher, than their surroundings, typically enclosing lines or groups of raised dots as well. These are leaf scars. The shape of the scar is unique to each tree species, and corresponds to the shape of the bottom of the leaf stem. The raised dots are remnants of the veins that once coursed through the stem like so many freight lines, connecting the leaf's green islands to the energy-consuming mainland. You may even, if you're lucky, and the wind hasn't confused the issue, find on the ground a leaf whose stem bottom matches the leaf scar.

The scar is a testament to the tree's prescience.

The tree, having anticipated the loss of its leaf, created a place where separation could occur, and limited the effect of the loss to that site. As the leaf began slowing down its energy production, the tree established a zone of severance, or abscission, where it actively weakened cells around the base of the stem. The stem began to tear away, a few cells at a time, while the tree sealed the wound against infection. In the end, the leaf was only held on by the most fragile of tethers; a breeze, a raindrop, or a wandering squirrel were too much for it, and it fell.

Having fallen, a leaf is redeemed. It decomposes into soil, which nourishes the tree. The tree will incorporate nutrients from the fallen leaf to enable it to grow, transforming the leaf back into the tree that gave it form and reason for existence.

Having fallen, the leaf cannot be put back. No matter whether the leaf scar and stem end match perfectly: try as you might, you can't re-attach them.

Though tree and leaf are no longer attached, tree and leaf are inextricably connected. Attachment entails the acceptance of non-attachment to what must change. Attachment therefore means letting go, healing, and beginning again. Connection, on the other hand, is the apprehension of what does not change: the form of the tree, the cycle of seasons, the life-giving power of light. Maintaining connection requires incorporating the essence of the relationship and generating new forms of it. If the tree didn't let the leaf go, it would crumble into dust, its nutrients lost. Only by letting go, at the right time, can connectedness be maintained.

Connection subsists in the never-ending process of change that underlies every life. The scar is evidence that there was an attachment: even more, that there was a past.

It is a fixed image of what was, like the memory of a farewell wave.

Pick-up Sticks

Late fall: warm days and cool nights alternate with cold days and icy nights; moist air and unstable weather create rain, fog, mist and storms. Tearing through the treetops, wind flings branches onto the ground where they lie in scattered debris piles, littering the leaf layers that cap the woodland humus.

It's the time of year for festive gatherings of friends and family around the table. Here are the fruits of an abundant harvest, logs afire in the hearth, the reflected glow of uplifted faces.

Outside, in the woods, beauty hides its face to the ground. Splashed on the underside of a fallen tree branch are patches of color and texture. The patches compose a mosaic from afar, but each piece is its own work of art when viewed at close range.

Against a striated brown bark background made glossy by the damp, are dots of white. Magnified, they reveal themselves to be feathery cups an eighth-inch in diameter. The interior surface of each one is splined and ciliated, decorated like an etched crystal goblet. These are the mushrooms known as common split-gills, the most widespread fungi on earth. They have the remarkable ability to dry out and rehydrate their cup-shaped fruiting bodies as conditions warrant, and so they may appear at any time of the year. But the clusters of elegant drinking vessels seem especially appropriate at this season.

Traversing the surface of the tree branch are quarter-inch long slender white worms, as delicate as angel-hair pasta. Up close, they are not merely white but are in fact translucent. Visible within their tubular interior are clumps of minute brown or white specks, the remnants of previous meals. Enchytraeid worms (also called pot worms), which dwell in the soil and leaf duff, subsist on a diet of fungi and bacteria. In the process of foraging and eating, they transport organic matter around the soil and leaf layers, and excavate tunnels in the soil that enable air and water to permeate throughout it. Wriggling across the branch, their segmented bodies contract and expand: specks within lines within tubes – like a freight train, seen from above, traveling slowly through a wheat field.

Pink circles spot the branch here and there, like calamine lotion on poison ivy. Magnified, they assume the shape and texture of sea anemones, with shaggy white outer circles topped by round-tipped gelatinous-looking cylinders. The color deepens from light pink at the outside to orange and coral in the middle. These are radiating phlebia, an ugly name for a pretty fungus. Fungi seem to attract names of contempt no matter how gorgeous their coloration or form. This particular species is one of the crust fungi (not very tempting that), and, even worse, it (like the split-gill) is a member of the "white rot" group. Beneath the bark surface, below the floristic disk that is its fruiting body, the phlebia is getting down to the serious business of digesting wood. Deep within the tree's cell walls, long chains of lignin – the complex polymer that helps to strengthen woody plants – block the fungus's access to cellulose, which it uses as a source for nutritious carbon. Like a human who will gladly endure the arduous labor of breaking apart a crab shell to get at the succulent meat inside, the phlebia and its fellow white-rot gourmets will sunder the tough lignin to obtain the white cellulose. This voracious appetite has endeared white-rot fungi to the paper-pulping and bleaching industries, which seek benign alternatives to processes that create massive amounts of toxic byproducts. Meanwhile the much older industry of recycling deadwood into soil nutrients for growing plants goes on at its own pace, quietly creating beauty as a byproduct.

Driftwood, whose form is wrought by the wind and waves, conveys a sense of the natural forces that created it even when it is taken from the seashore and placed in a window. Not so with this tree branch. Remove it from the soil on which it rests, change the light and the moisture conditions, and it will be transformed from a substrate for beauty into a mere stick. Leave it where it is, and given time, the branch will disappear, turned into food for future tree branches. To find this kind of beauty, pick up sticks – but to keep it, put them back.

a long the riverrun

In Bucks County, we live in the midst of a great conversation that we call the Delaware Valley. To hear it, float down the river that gives its name to our region.

The Delaware River begins in Hancock, New York, where its East and West branches converge (an area known to its inhabitants, oddly enough, as "the" Delaware Valley). For the next 330 miles, until it empties into the Delaware Bay at Cape May Point, the river encounters no dams or other impoundments. Thus, although many of its 216 tributaries (as well as both of its originating branches) are checked by reservoirs, and although must pass around obstructions such as wing dams and bridge abutments, the Delaware lays claim to be the longest free-flowing river east of the Mississippi (the Yellowstone, its western counterpart, is twice as long).

The general shape of its course is familiar to anyone who, having attended grade school in Pennsylvania, was taught to draw a state map bordered on the east with a pair of vertical waves. The first of these waves crests at Matamoras, PA, where the river makes a right-angle turn to follow the edge of the Allegheny Front along a finger of Blue Mountain.

Hello, I must be going, says River to Rock.
I'll be here when you get back, says Rock to River.

The second wave crests at Pennsbury, where the Proprietor built a house high on the riverbank, looking back toward his homeland. The trough between these two waves is the south-tending course that begins at Easton and ends at Durham. It is here, as it enters Bucks County, that the river makes a decisive turn as it meets an impassable wall of diabase rock, the product of an ancient volcano. This was lava that ran like water.

I pity you, says River to Rock. Once, you could glide over the Earth, like me, making your own way. Now, you are stuck here, receiving visitors, waiting for news. Oh, says Rock to River, your time will come. You will slow, you will harden, you will witness the future passing in front of you and floating away, just beyond your reach.

As if bowing in deference, the river alters its course here, bending to run nearly due east until the diabase disappears. Then it wends its way back. By the time it reaches Erwinna, the river is once again heading south. From here to Point Pleasant it is a broad, shallow reach,

Fall

possessed of a steady, sure current, and cradled by tree-covered undeveloped shorelines. The Trenton "Falls" – rocky shoals – form a natural barrier to commercial traffic upstream. All in all, then, this is a fine stretch for an afternoon of kayaking.

Today the river is clear enough to watch the cobbled bottom unwind below our boats like a nubbly ribbon. Occasionally, huge flat submerged boulders reveal their existence by coaxing a subtle change in the river's surface texture: from diffusely calm to tautly smooth. The wide sky and the wide water reflect the hot sun; cool refreshing water spritzes from our circling paddles. Now high red shale formations tower over us on the New Jersey side...Devil's Tea Table, Tumble Falls. The rocks are deeply incised with ledges; each layer is the bed of a primeval inland waterway. The passage of time is caught in the physical structure of the rocks. Below the rocks, the river passes, endlessly passing, always current, always now. Yet the water we float on was just someone else's now, someone far upstream. And soon it will be someone else's now, downstream.

River cannot bear to pass by Rock without taking a bit along. So Rock flows, crumb by crumb, downstream, into the future. Sometimes River is too ambitious, breaking off larger chunks of Rock than River can bear away. These big pieces of Rock sojourn in the River, and they make the River sing. The song is a shooshroar. River gets to stop, and leap high in the air like Rock does in its cliffs and ledges. Rock stands aloof, watching. It was young once, and mud. Full of teeming life that slipped and crawled and scuttled, and which left its footprints, its shells and its skeletons in Rock so Rock could remember what it was like when water was high, and Rock was low.

So far, the wind has laid low; now a chill breeze begins to blow against the current, rippling the river surface in lines perpendicular to the banks. A wash of gray clouds, uniform, flat and gray, like a screenful of lint, advances from the southwest. Drumroll, lights, action. The first raindrops feel like spray, ignorable. Then spattering, noise like sizzling oil as they accelerate and the storm drives in. To the shore! Lifeless, timeless, reliable rock.

Sky says, you, River, I know you. You have left fragments of yourself with me. I thank you for the gift of time, and I return them to you. And Sky sings, with a barkclang, of its return of River's gift.

The rain is cold. It pours down for fifteen minutes; we are drenched to the skin. But it is only water. And afterwards when we put in again, the river is warm. Why is rain cool and River warm?

No says Sky, you have it wrong. I am cool, cool blue, and River brings me warmth of the sun.

Rock is still. Rock has known warmth, a long time ago.

River says, hello, I must be going.

Winter

Cries of the Heart

The owlet's cries started in the late spring: a piercing squawk, rising in pitch, repeated every fifteen seconds. Sometimes the call was so loud that it seemed to be right outside the window, sometimes so faint that I could not be sure it wasn't two branches rubbing together in the distance. On summer evenings we'd sit on the front porch and listen as the sound bounced around like the ball in a squash court: now it's to the left, now it's across the street, now it's overhead, now to the left again.

The young great horned owl issues these begging calls as it pleads with its parents for food. The owlets are typically born in March, and remain unable to feed themselves for months. Mom and Dad owl are kept busy night after night, hunting down voles, mice, rabbits and other delectables. Occasionally we'll find the evidence of a meal at the base of a tree in the front yard: fur and bones and teeth compacted into a pellet like the compressed remains of a car at the scrapyard.

We began spotting the owlet at the same time the crows did, in late summer. Perched on a high branch, it would remain oblivious to the mobbing calls as the crows circled all around and landed on adjacent trees, while never directly attacking it. After a few minutes of unrelenting harassment, the owl might pick up and fly ten feet away, but that was all it would concede. Eventually the crows would tire of the standoff and move on.

The cries continued as fall arrived. The owlet was easier to spot, now: with fewer leaves to hide behind, the odd lump on a tree limb was that much more obvious.

Some evenings it would call when it was still light out, as if it were hoping to bring dusk on faster.

One day in early November I noticed a flurry of movement in the backyard. There was the owlet, devouring a two-foot-long garter snake. It was high noon. An odd time for a night hunter to be out, for sure, but at least the young owl seemed to be learning to feed itself. Or perhaps this was the owl equivalent of mac-and-cheese out of the box at midnight, what the college freshman scarfs down and calls dinner when mom's not around to cook the real thing.

Two weeks later, we woke up at 4 a.m. to watch the Leonid meteor shower. As we lay flat on the cold ground, staring up at green and blue sparks racing across the sky, we heard the owl's cries. I was reminded of another celestial event that I had observed from our front porch, the total lunar eclipse in January 2000. Just as the moon had begun to be obscured by the shadow of the Earth, a great horned owl had started hooting in the tree above. The hooting continued as the moon gradually disappeared, and at the eclipse's peak, when the moon could only be seen as an amber aura around a dark central disk, the owl took off out of the tree and flew into the woods. Was it disturbed by the change in the normal order? Thrilled by the unusual light? Or simply going about its business, with the eclipse merely a coincidence?

This November morning, as the owlet continued to squawk, a cow joined in with deep, slow *moos*. One called, the other answered. The meteors traced sizzling lines overhead. Each sound and sight was an opening to dimensions of our world that we know only briefly, lit superficially by these momentary flashes.

After that morning, nights were silent. That is as it should be: eventually the young owl must make its own home and fend for itself. Owls travel as much as twenty miles after leaving the nest, to find new territory. Even so, half of all great horned owls die in their first year alone – of starvation.

January darkness resounds now with the "who-cooks-for-you" hooting of the adult owl, seeking a mate. And that is as it should be. Yet one evening, when I step outside to listen for it, I hear, faintly on the wind, a rising squawk. Is it the prodigal child, back so soon? Is this a cry for help? *I'm not ready for this. I still need you. The world is so big.*

Did I hear an owl at all?

Night and Day

The first full moon of the New Year dressed for the occasion, donning an iridescent diamond-studded chiffon gown. Clouds parted before her beauty, leaving the black velvet stage for Herself alone.

Next morning when she awoke on the other side of the sky, her fancy dress rumpled and soiled, old Sun had already started the fire in the grate. He gathered a puffy white comforter around him, and then spread it high against the ceiling like an egret unfolding its wings. The flames cast red, orange and yellow hues onto the underside of the blanket. Sun danced a little dance to a Cole Porter tune. "Your time has come and gone," he called to Moon. "I am as constant as constant can be, whereas you can only be counted on to shine once in a while."

Moon cried tears of rage. Great big drops rolled down her plump cheeks; she shook her head and they sprayed far and wide. Then she set about sobbing some more. She blew her nose long and loud, over and over, till shutters rattled and trees toppled. Moon's tears filled the sky. They soaked the Sun's quilt, soaked it good, and Sun went into his room and shut the door. He didn't come out till Moon had cried herself to sleep.

Well, now, that is one explanation. And here is another.

The better you know someone, the more you recognize those little signs that mean things are not what they seem. A perfectly placid disposition, the exemplar of cheerful optimism, is belied by the persistent tic that others mistake for a happy-go-lucky wink. The frown of concentration differs by an eyebrow-hair's breadth from the frown of annoyance. And a clear, crisp winter's night with a brilliant full moon portends a day of wet weather if the moon is wearing a halo. That happens when the moon is shining through a curtain of high-altitude cirrus and cirrostratus clouds, which are composed of small hexagonal ice crystals that, like prisms, bend (refract) the moonlight at a 22-degree angle, into a cone. We see the cone end-on, as a ring. It can be white, or if conditions are right, a spectrum: reddish on the inside to violet on the outside. The clouds are high enough and thin enough to be virtually invisible to us on the ground, and transparent to stars and planets.

Those high-altitude night clouds are being driven ahead of a mass of low-pressure air approaching from the west. Moisture builds up where it meets the colder, drier air. By daybreak, clouds have thickened and lowered, while the air layer below is still dry and the eastern horizon, ahead of the disturbance, remains clear. Light from the rising sun is reflected downward by the clouds. The light is bounced back through the clear air before it has had a chance to reach the higher atmosphere, where dust and moisture would scatter the light and turn it blue. The result is a vibrant, sky-filling sunrise, all plum and apricot and peach: winter painting with the palette of summer preserves. Eventually, the low-pressure storm system presaged by the clouds sweeps in, bringing wind and precipitation.

Which you can condense into "Red sky at morning, sailors take warning," and "Ring around the moon, rain or snow is coming soon."

But try telling that to Moon. She won't listen. She's out getting her gown cleaned for the next Big Night.

A Winter's Tale

When robins re-appear, spring can't be far behind, right? The winter-weary exuberance with which we greet the season is reflected in the word-pictures we use for the robin. The red-red-robin's bob-bob-bobbin', its "cheerily cheerily cheer-up" song, and its eagerness to arise at dawn and be the "early bird that gets the worm" are so familiar as to be part of our folklore. Few of us drink spring tonics made from fresh shoots of wild nettles; a few more of us take note of the appearance of sleepy groundhogs just out of hibernation; but even as rural countryside gives way to suburbia, and our direct experience of many seasonal associations has faded, the robin-spring link remains stubbornly stuck in our cultural memory: this is one message from nature that even lawn-lubbers heed.

The robin's story is comfortingly circular. A typical bird joins up with others in late summer and autumn; huge flocks fly south for the winter. They hang out there eating berries and other fruits. As winter wanes, earthworms return to the top layers of newly warmed soil, so robins follow the 37°F isotherm north with the spring. They settle onto their breeding grounds in March, build nests and raise families over the summer when earthworms and insects are plentiful for feeding to young, then in the autumn head south again. Winter dormancy alternates with spring awakening; our little life is rounded by a sleep.

It's a familiar story, and for the typical robin, a true one. But it doesn't cover all the evidence. It's like taking an oath by putting your hand over a bag of popcorn: turn the bag over and some kernels of a different truth drop out. As dusk fell one day in early January, hundreds of robins descended into the wooded areas in back of my house. Some of the birds snatched bright red berries from the bittersweet vines. Others scratched at the ground, tossing leaves and dirt over their heads with abandon and pecking at the exposed soil, looking for all the world like they were hunting insects and earthworms. The next morning, a hearty "cheerily cheerily cheerup" pealed out from a white pine tree as the sun's rays tipped its needles with gold. Robins? In Bucks County? In January? What's the story?

We like to make stories out of what we see; we create the world anew by telling tales. The tale of the typical robin not only makes sense, it matches what we observe – most of the time. Yet, for the all-too-typical robin, there are some disadvantages to following the standard story line. For one thing, there are a lot of robins in the world. The most abundant bird species in Pennsylvania, robins are much more numerous now than when William Penn arrived. Suburban landscaping preferences, especially lawns and shrubs, supply them with food and nesting habitat that the forests and farms of centuries ago did not. With so much success, migrant hordes of birds in the southern wintering ranges increase the pressure on food resources. Birds who stay behind, or just lag the trend, face less competition for available food and water. (On the other hand, there is also less available – not to mention the hazards of cold, snow and ice, which increase the birds' energy needs and at the same time make fuel harder to find.) As a result of global warming, average temperatures are higher up north than in past years – high enough even in January to find insects and earthworms if the conditions are right. Too, cold is relative: our area is downright balmy compared with, say, Labrador, so robins from the far north sometimes venture here to bask in what is the southern part of their winter range.

The standard story is neat and tidy, has the ring of eternity about it, and is not fundamentally untrue. Yet we should not mistake the standard for the exclusive. Press your robin-shaped cookie cutter into a sheet of dough, and you get a lot of nice neat robin cookies; in between is what doesn't fit into the cookie cutter, but that doesn't mean it's not the stuff of which robins are made. A robin in March makes a story of spring. A robin in January makes a story of winter. Winter's stripped landscape makes opportunity that much more thrilling: see the flash of a berry and seize it, cull the earth's temporary bounty produced by a warm spell. Sing from a tree while yours is the only voice, even if you're also the only audience. Surprise someone. Inspire them to write a new story.

Frozen Time

From there to here, then to now, birth to death, we keep going, on and on. We experience a kinetic time: time that we perceive as propulsion, moving ever forward, carrying us with it. Eventually we wind down and stop. But by then it's too late. The world – time – goes on without us.

Living beings have failed miserably to wrest time out of its relentless flow, freeze it, and examine it from all angles. Oddly, that is the province of liquid things, of streams and rivers, lava flows and mudslides.

There is a place nearby where, in deepest, coldest, bluest winter, you can encounter stopped time. Go to Ringing Rocks County Park, in Bridgeton Township. Skirt the justly famed boulder field – leave it for another season. Continue on the wide, rocky woods trail. After a few hundred yards, the dense deciduous woods dissolves into spacious light, feathered by tall hemlocks. The trail gives out to an immense swath of dark boulders.

Below the moat of boulders is a flat-bottomed gorge. Tilting toward you, it's rimmed with jumbled rocks on the low side and sloping bluffs on the far side. Along, between, and over the rocks, water runs. Falls Creek has cut this ravine into the steeply rounded hillside the way a baker might have slashed a plump, rising loaf of raisin bread.

The origin of the creek's name becomes evident as you look upstream, where the ravine seems to have been dislocated upwards. Along a cliff-face, 30 feet high, appears to be a portico with immense translucent columns, crystalline shutters and glistening alabaster swag. This three-story mansion is High Falls, the highest waterfall in Bucks County. Frozen now, only a thin trickle of water flows underneath the icy gingerbreading.

Clamber over the boulders to stand at the base of the waterfall. In spring, the noise of the falling water would be deafening. Now, a damp chill takes its place. The cold seems to suck warmth out of the air the way the cacophony of falling water vacuums up silence.

Behind the ice, along the cliff face itself, layers of reddish-brown rock are stacked like Ry-Krisps. At the falls' base, ice forms thin top sheets in shallows, etched in intricate patterns. At the margin of the tilting ravine shelf and the low creek bank, massive frosted boulders lie in piles like the abandoned cookies of a giant toddler.

You can, if you're restless, walk across the ravine above the falls, and look down the immense gash, then continue on to the other side. A trail also leads along the ravine on the near side. The ravine bottom itself is flat and easily traversed even by dogs and children.

Or just stand still. Be with time stilled in the rocks. Be with time stilled in the ice.

Frozen in the flat red rocks – Brunswick shale – are the courses of rivers that flowed 150-250 million years ago. Sediments eroded from the highlands washed into the waterways, swirled and settled. Layer upon layer, bed upon bed, the sediments built up, were buried, and lithified.

Frozen in the dark boulders – igneous diabase – is the intrusion into the orderly layered sedimentary world of molten volcanic magma. It erupted through crevices and flowed over the shale layers. As it did so, the magma baked the shale, and, like the top of a loaf of bread, cracked it. The sheet of molten lava cooled and hardened into diabase. Over eons, it fragmented into blocks, and then into boulders. Meanwhile the creek was cutting down through the hillside: scouring the layers of soft shale, one by one.

The baked shale offered more resistance, thus becoming the bed for still flowing water: as it is now and was then.

Frozen in the ice is falling water, interrupted in its inexorable adaptation to circumstance. Flowing or stopping, rushing or pooling, water does not so much seek its own level as accept the level that it is given. Frozen, it reveals the conditions it last experienced, limning temperature, height, velocity with visible form; stopping the temporary and making it – for the time being – permanent.

Are you still standing at the frozen falls? Tarry not, lest you too be stilled. For humans, time goes on.

Of Bark and a Bird

Up close, the furrowed bark of a mature red oak is no less impressive than the Rockies. Deep valleys alternate with rough ridges; ragged peaks, topped with green outcroppings, jut out above the crests. This is a textured landscape that is as picturesque as any view from an airplane – and no reservations are required. The intrepid explorer who circumnavigates the tree with a magnifying lens will find contrasts in climate as distinct as the differences between northern and southern hemispheres. On the sun-facing side, the bark is dry and scaly with lichens; a few inches away, habitually shaded furrows are lined with moss. Equally dramatic is the vertical variation from lofty heights, where winter's driving snow coats the ridgetops and cobwebs are strung from peak to peak like the cables of tiny trams, to barren desert-like depths, where moisture never penetrates.

Bark is tree tissue long past living, yet its surface, like the unliving rock surface of our Earth, supports life forms that depend on it for food and shelter. Some, like the moss and lichens, are visible, but others are hidden. Tucked within gaps in the bark, insects and spiders sit out the winter in cave-like cracks. Wind, water and weather pass them by.

Not so the needle-like beak of the brown creeper. Like a dentist's cleaning pick, it curves down, so as to fit into tight spaces. No huddled arthropod is safe from this probe; the bird extricates a meal with the precision of a surgeon.

There is little to distinguish the bird from the bark. The brown creeper wears a drab striped coat of few colors: a palate of wood and shadow. As winter light slants across a tree trunk, fissures in the bark paint the tree with patches of gray, black and brown – patches that look just like the perched brown creeper clinging to the tree trunk. As the bird moves up in a spiral, stopping to poke into crevices, these striped patches move, but subtly, as when sunlight flits across the tree trunk.

Foraging from tree to tree, the brown creeper is in constant prepositional motion – winding up and around a trunk, then flying over and down to the base of the next tree to begin the up and around again. Not just any tree will do: it must be mature enough to have developed the bark furrows that harbor food in the form of insects, larvae and eggs. The bird's breeding habitat is even more specific: it nests in a clump of moss tucked between a flap of bark and the tree trunk. This is a bird made for bark.

It is not until a tree has lived long enough to have developed those interesting wrinkles that are the prizes of age that it can support the bird. Young trees are too shallow, their bark smooth and unscarred. The skin of an old tree is marked by experience. It is tattooed with black streaks left by lightning strikes, pocked with pinholes drilled by beetles and cavities excavated by woodpeckers, gashed where storm-torn limbs have slammed against the tree trunk. Old bark strengthens the tree. The corrugated creases covering the old oak, the knitted rows wrapping the hickory, the cross-hatching of the maple and the rutted roads lining the elm, all buttress the tree as it ages, grows more stout and loses its flexibility.

Yet age gives rise not only to sturdiness but also to lightness. The brown creeper, a patch of bark flitting from tree to tree, is like an emissary made of the tree's own skin. As the creeper moves about the forest, the tree gives up a bit of itself to its neighbors, and receives them in kind. For brief moments, it is suspended in air, neither here nor there. Through the travels of the brown creeper, the tree is liberated from its rooted existence.

Here is a bird born from a bark shelter, and nourished by the bark bounty. Its coat simulates the tree's outerwear. Bark has created the brown creeper in its own image. And it is good.

Snowmelt and Memory

The first snowfall of the season blew in overnight, covering the landscape with an inch of frosting that softened the jagged outlines of recently bare branches. The snow disappeared almost as soon as the morning was over, washed away by the rain and then melted by the sun.

Days later, though, there are still bits of snow remaining. They are remnants of the whole, reminding us of what was so fleetingly here. There are snow smudges on the ground on the north side of trees, where the sun doesn't shine. Isolated drifts stripe the farm fields, packed by wind into plough-rows. Patches cling to the steep berms in roadside ditches.

Out of one of those ditches, a passing car flushes a flock of rotund juncos, some gray, some brown. The white on their outer tail feathers is like a piece of that snow patch they've caught and can't shake off.

In southeastern Pennsylvania, juncos are heralds of the snow season. They arrive in mid-autumn from their breeding grounds, as far north as the Arctic circle, wearing that snow-patch like a talisman of their salad days. They stick around through winter, on into spring, long after one would think they should be on their way, like the last bit of unmelted snow tucked under a layer of leaves beside a tree root.

Then one day in April, they're not here. When was the last time I saw them? A day, two days, a week? It is the fact of their absence that creates the memory of their having been here. Otherwise I would have no need for the memory. So how do I know what to remember? Did it take a few years of seeing the juncos, then not seeing them, to know I should notice them, so I could fix them in my memory for when they're gone?

When I was growing up in suburban Philadelphia in the 1960's we had many more snow days, and deeper snowfalls, than we do now. Whether it is global warming, or cyclical weather patterns, or a combination of the two, there is less snow than there used to be. I remember some of those snowfalls: I remember rolling snowmen and building snowforts, sledding on wooden sleds with red metal runners, and snow cascading over the tops of my rubber snow boots. At least I think I remember: I may be helped along by the home movies that fixed my memories as grainy, silent scenes in a frame.

Last year, the first snow was the last snow of the season, not that we knew it at the time. My son put a snowball in the freezer. Over the course of the dry, snowless winter we would open the freezer for something else, and the snowball was a tangible reminder of the snow. It got smaller and smaller as it evaporated (accelerated by the defrost cycle). Eventually it was gone, melted into memory.

You can't see snow melting, and you can't see memories forming. You can see the white tailfeathers of a little round bird, though. They remind you to remember.

True Friends

"A friend," wrote Ralph Waldo Emerson, "may well be reckoned the masterpiece of Nature."

Emerson, of course, was describing the intricacies of interpersonal relationships, the balance of likes and opposites, strengths and weaknesses, that combine to make a bond between two people. This deep, primitive instinct is one of the defining characteristics of our species. Alone, none of us could survive, but together we flourish.

At the core of friendship is the appreciation of the value of an individual.

One winter several years ago, the airport in Quakertown, PA, announced that it had hired a team of horses to clear trees from an 18-acre parcel of wetlands.

The trees, it seems, were potential safety hazards to the adjacent runway, and had to be cut down. Heavy equipment could damage the wetlands, so instead, horses dragged felled logs to a waiting chipper. The airport manager noted that the work was being done in an "environmentally friendly" manner.

Giving the airport management due credit for protecting wetlands, can logging – even horse-drawn logging – be described as friendly?

Up the road from where I live stands a wild black cherry tree. Here, about a quarter of a mile before the road bends over the ridge, houses on acre lots peter out into farm fields, pastures and woods. Dozens of cherry trees line both sides of the road, mixed in with pine, hemlock and spruce and an occasional oak or walnut. Gnarled grape vines, some as thick as my forearm, twist through the branches and drape over the trunks.

Years ago, this tree – like its companions – got its start when a bird, perched on the telephone wires strung along the road, dropped a seed into the cleared area below. Today the tree is about sixty feet tall. From a base about two feet in diameter, it rises in two trunks each a foot wide that curve gently away from each other. The gray bark is furrowed and broken into pieces whose edges are curled up, exposing an inner red. Along with its height and girth, the bark indicates this is a mature tree: younger specimens retain the characteristic horizontal lines on the bark of the cherry family. The wild cherry is the largest of our native cherry trees, its wood prized for furniture, but outside of a forest, the trees are typically too small and twisted to be of much value to the cabinetmaker.

About ten feet up one trunk is a hole an inch-and-a-half wide, where a limb was long ago pruned by the electric company, a passing truck, or the wind. With binoculars, one can see that it has been dug out and enlarged: the yellow-brown wood is furrowed with sharp indented lines.

On a snowy, blowy January day, I am taking a walk past the tree. I hear a churr-churrr-churr from above and behind. I look up, into the driving wind; snowflakes sting my face. A red squirrel scampers from a nearby white pine, takes a short leap onto the cherry tree and skitters down it, then scoots into the hole and disappears.

Red squirrels are not nearly as common in our area as the familiar gray squirrel. Tiny, loudly territorial and unmistakably red, they prefer a diet of pine nuts, so red squirrels are typically found in coniferous or mixed woods. Unlike the gray squirrel, whose leafy nests perch on tree limbs, they often nest in tree cavities. They do not bury their nuts in the ground, but cache them in a log or a tree hollow.

The wind has been blowing snow all day. Snow coats the windward side of the cherry tree trunk. The squirrel's hole is on the opposite side, protected from the elements.

The squirrel pops its head out of the hole just far enough to observe me. The hole frames the squirrel's head. Round black eyes stare at me impassively. Snowflakes whip past. Snug inside, the squirrel is sixty feet tall and invincible, in a suit of armor. Secure within the bonds of friendship.

Winter Remainder

Four seasons correspond neatly to four arithmetic operations. Spring, of course, is addition, when getting together is all the rage. Summer's warming oven creates the conditions for proliferation, of multiplication. Autumn, when families scatter and the young go off to form their own households, is division.

Winter is subtraction. The sensible world is stripped to its essence. Trees are laid bare. Insects remove themselves from the air and burrow underground; turtles abandon the pond surface and sink into mud bottom. Heat recedes; cold winds blow away dust and water vapor, leaving the night sky a velvet background for the constellations. Brilliant fall colors flee, leaving the dun shades, gray and brown. When it falls, snow takes away sound, sharp edges, and surface detail; the earth, pillowed in crystalline down, sleeps.

Thus scraped down to the bone, the skeleton of the world is revealed in the details that add up to a whole. Under a January crescent moon at midnight, the frozen ground reflects a faint silvery light, rendering every object the color of shadow. It is a hard cold, without the softening effect of humidity: the kind of cold that creates a crisp surrounding silence – not snow-muffled, but clear. Into the silence the sudden skittering of a dried leaf on the roof is like a shout. The trees begin to sway, the tips of their unadorned branches rustling as they rub together. Only then do I feel the breeze on my cheeks.

Shorn of leaves, the tree branches seem to stretch skyward. Stars play peek-a-boo between the spread fingers of the forking boughs. Through binoculars, the incomprehensible distance between us is reduced to intimacy, as if Arcturus and Rigel perch just over the next ridge.

A bark, a shuffling footstep. The night gives up one of its gray-brown shadows, then two, then three. Deer promenade slowly across the yard, pausing every few steps to swivel their heads around. I shrink back into the darkness, hunker down and wrap my gray coat around me while I spy at them through the binoculars. Their exhalations puff out in silver-tipped clouds that linger around their noses. I try to hold my own breath, knowing they will sense it immediately. One of the group, the largest of the three, walks with a pronounced limp, almost falling to the ground every time the left front foot moves forward. How long has she survived, thus marked for death?

The trees sway, the moon sneaks a glimpse through the branches and its reflection catches the binocular lenses. The deer freeze in their tracks. I know I'm caught, but I don't give up. I lower the binoculars. We stare at each other for a moment through the moonglow; then they bound off, crashing through the underbrush.

Winter subtracts our ease, the comforting, mediating surfaces that constitute our experience of the world. It leaves us face to face with what we cannot know.

Nothing Doing

High above the cattail sea, they sit. There is nothing else worth doing at the moment.

Not sloth, nor indolence, but the imperative of refraining from action when action is not called for, saturates the Quakertown Swamp.

Two miles southeast of Quakertown, Bog Run meanders eastward on its way to the Tohickon Creek. Unlike typical valley-bottom streams, the margin between the flow and its surroundings is indistinct: of a piece with mud and mire that extends in all directions.

Water has made a grudging peace with rocks that will not give any of themselves here. A solid sheet of impermeable diabase is perched above the main groundwater aquifer, frustrating the surface water's attempts to seep into the earth. So the water eddies, lingers, and pools above the rock layer.

Slowly settling within the liquid are solid bits of sloughed-off organic matter and slow-slurried gravel: the dead and departed, worn and weathered, now become sediment and silt. A fine substrate for muck-loving plants like rushes, cattails, willows, tussock sedges, buttonbush, and swamp rose.

At 518 acres the biggest inland wetlands in Bucks County – inundating parts of East Rockhill, West Rockhill, and Richland Townships – the Swamp is the breeding grounds for 91 different species of birds. Great Blue Herons have established the largest rookery in eastern Pennsylvania here.

Late March through April is the best time to visit the colony, because the herons have begun nesting and the roost trees have yet to leaf out to block your view. The birds build their large, shaggy nests, made of sticks and lined with grasses, at the tops of trees. Marsh mud acts as a moat to deter tree-climbing predators like raccoons.

It keeps people away too. So do the Posted signs: other than some pieces of state game land, much of the Swamp is privately owned. But it's not necessary to get your feet wet and muddy, or risk a trespassing citation, on a swamp trek. You can easily stand and observe the herons from Muskrat Road, which bisects the swamp.

Even better, scramble up the railroad embankment from nearby Rich Hill Road. Only one of the two tracks is active; the other gets traffic but not often. Walk north. Hopping the ties, teetering on the rusty rails, or trudging over the gravel, you're above the marsh, but still immersed in its character.

A culvert where the stream flows under the tracks is a good flat spot to sit. Look west over the cattail waves. Herons are silhouetted in the trees, as if the slanting sun had etched them into the sky.

The herons are sitting. You are sitting.

It's not so easy to sit. Stillness is a discipline; restlessness the natural condition. Energy builds up and needs to be dissipated. Occasionally a sitting heron may stretch its long neck, spread its pterodactyl wings, or unfold its stilt legs.

Behind you, on the unused tracks, is a gathering of empty boxcars. Rolling stock with nowhere to roll: iron and steel fused, molded and shaped into useful objects. Without a current use, though, they have lost their meaning. There is nothing to do. So they've been shunted off to a side track until a new use comes along.

The railcars are sitting. You are sitting. The herons are sitting.

As the herons sit and wait with their eggs, things happen of their own accord. Cells nourished by their surroundings divide, become new shapes, and find new uses, ready to do something. Something comes of doing nothing.

Sitting, you may let your mind slow down, linger and eddy. Settle the clutter and let the sediment of your surroundings swirl around and become a substrate for something new. Here is as good a place as any.

Perchance to Dream

Quiet lies over the meadow. No breeze disturbs the tall stands of dried goldenrod, their gold now turned to shades of russet, mahogany, and sepia. Leaves long ago fallen, flowers become seedcases, pliable stalks stiff shafts, solidago awaits winter's end.

Peace there is not. Into the bright blue dome of silence resounds a sharp rapping: a tap-tap-tapping. Knock-knock-knocking, a downy woodpecker probes for a doorway into the rounded gall atop the goldenrod stem.

Within the heart of the eurosta fly larva, does a chill settle? For inside the gall – the swollen ball of distended goldenrod tissue, once green and now hardened into a brown globe – a larva rests: having eaten its fill of fresh plant matter during the summer, it has entered diapause, a kind of suspended animation. Metabolism has slowed, respiration has halted, cells have filled with antifreeze: the ungiving outside world matters not at all for now. Not till the longer, warmer days of spring cue it to return to a wakened world will the larva return to its metamorphic course, to pupate before finally emerging as an adult.

The larva, plump as a grain of risotto rice, is surrounded by spongy plant tissue: the leftovers from its summer meal. Before settling in for the long winter, the larva excavated an upsloping tunnel right up to the inside of the gall's thin skin. After pupation, the new adult fly will inflate a balloon-like structure in its forehead against this outermost epidermal layer, breaking the membrane open and enabling the fly to escape.

During winter, the dark, paper-thin skin covers the exit. Thus there must be a faint light shining into the larval bedchamber. Comfort through the long night? Or a simple clock, measuring the parabolic progress of the day-night ratio, until spring sounds the alarm?

Peck. Peck. Peck. Like a carpenter checking for studs, the downy woodpecker is tapping over the upper third of the gall, listening for the void that says, larva door here. (A doorless gall is inhabited by a dead eurosta larva, or one whose den has been taken over by the larva of an even smaller insect – and to the woodpecker, an unappetizing one at that – a parasitic wasp that, having hatched from an egg deposited through the gall walls, has eaten the fly larva.)

The light goes out. In its place, the tip of the woodpecker's bill, breaking the seal. Now it is probing, chiseling out the walls, widening the escape hatch. Coming closer.

The larva sleeps on. That is what it does now, and no amount of pounding on its bedroom door can waken it. It hearkens only to the sweet call of spring.

With a final stab, the woodpecker breaks through the eurosta's protective cover. The chisel now a forceps, the bird's beak closes around the tender morsel. The woodpecker jerks its head back.

The eurosta exits, not when its own plan had dictated, but according to the agenda followed by the woodpecker.

For an instant, between gall and gullet, between the chamber of sleep and sleep eternal, does it see a flash of light?

Hold that Thought

Winter marches along, rank and file of cold nights following cold days, each dressed in fatigues: drab brown earth cloaked in ashen skies. Spring seems to come out of nowhere, a ker*boink*! Blossoms blooming, foliage unfurling, all creation a-borning. There it is, fully formed, like Pallas Athena, goddess of wisdom, from the head of Zeus. Like the unbidden flow of water from the ground. Like eternal hope.

Where does it come from, this sudden flowering, this startling verdancy? Where is the source of the new?

Look down on a warm winter day, a thaw day like a dream in which you open the door to a secret room where spring is closeted, putting on her gown. Under trees and thickets, tired old snowbanks, once powdery white and smooth, are now grizzled with ice and debris. Dark spots and speckles are scattered over the white crust. Just dirt? Bend closer. Here are leaf bits, insect parts, dust, seeds, and other detritus blown down from above, as if the trees were gargantuan whisk brooms that shake loose their sweepings in cleansing winds. After they land on the snow surface, the bits keep falling, but much more slowly. The dark debris absorbs sunlight reflected from its white surroundings, melting the snow around and under it, and it sinks down, down, down.

No hurry. Time to watch time passing. Sun warming the surface, snow melting in measured drips, counting time as the meltwater gathers itself at the tip of an ice crystal, the light glinting in prisms, surface tension and capillary action and gravity pulling the water into a drop

that falls with a languid regular beat. Drip. Drip. Drip.
Ker*boink*! What was that? Not a drip. A speckle spot. New
here, wasn't here before. Now – isn't here. It's over there.
No that's a spot of – ker*boink*! Gone.

Snow fleas.

Must be brief. Not much time between leaps.
They're not fleas. The snow part is right, but. They're a
species of springtails. Dirt speck size (1/8 inch).
Arthropods. Six legs, could be insects, could be just
relatives, depends on who you ask. Springtail experts don't
care. Too busy counting them. Millions, billions, trillions.
More springtails on planet than any other six-legged
creature. More springtails per square acre of prime soil
than there are people on planet (average soil: people in
China). Old too: fossils found from 400 million years ago.
(Pre-dinosaur time.) Scientific name: Colembolla. Means
glue-peg. Refers to appendage protruding from abdomen,
helps stick to leaves. Tricky scientists, ignoring locomotion.
Springing. No wings, short legs. How to move fast: unhook
tailspring prongs from catch under abdomen, Newton's first
law at work: tail springs back, body propelled forward up to
six inches ker*boink*!

Snow fleas.

They don't come from out of nowhere; rather they
climb up from under the snow. From their year-round
home, the layer of decaying leaves on the ground, they
travel up plant stems onto the snowbanks on warm winter
days, often swarming in large groups, on a mission to
reproduce or to migrate. Most types of soil-dwelling

springtails, despite their astonishing abundance, remain largely unknown to non-specialists: to any observer who lacks a screening apparatus and a magnifying lens they are effectively invisible. Of all the springtails, snow fleas are the ones most easily seen because they stand out against the white snow background. That is, they're easy to see, if you're looking for them.

They dance across the snow like letters on a page. The way words come out on paper, or paintings on a canvas, or brainstorms on a whiteboard. Onto the blank that isn't so new that it reflects all the light that hits it, but instead has seen a few freezes and a few melts, developed a crust and picked up some spots. Snow fleas come out of somewhere, not nowhere, but you have to be ready for them in order to spot them; otherwise they just look like pieces of dirt. Then as soon as you see them you have to know they'll be moving on, and catch sight of them before they go. Sure, you could look for them in the soil. You might even find them. Without the snow, though, they're not snow fleas. It's the snow that makes the snow fleas. The now that makes the new. A pre-condition to creation is not only knowing that the surprise will arrive, it's giving the surprise a place to occur. It's the winter that spring follows. A place to hold the thoughts, a blank page to see them against. It's the ker in ker*boink*.

Snowfates

Yes, the newspapers were right: snow was general all over Ireland. It was falling on every part of the dark central plain, on the treeless hills, falling softly upon the

Bog of Allen and, farther westward, softly falling into the dark mutinous Shannon waves.

But of course snow doesn't fall generally. It falls particularly. One flake at a time, falling on every part of the rolling valley, over the tree-fringed rock ridges, falling softly on the Quakertown Swamp and, farther westward, softly falling into the slow impassive Perkiomen currents.

And falling, snow falls snowflake by snowflake; not generally, but individually.

Each flake has a unique shape, the result of the fact that, as the consummate snow expositor Corydon Bell wrote, "ice crystallizing in the free atmosphere is a great improviser."

The snowflake forms as it falls, or more precisely forms by falling. Born as a droplet coalescing around a dust particle in a cloud, it takes its first shape — a hexagonal prism — as water vapor condenses on its surface. The prism's facets begin to sprout appendages as air currents juggle it from one temperature to another: now cold, now not-so-cold, now much colder. The temperatures and humidities that the growing crystal encounters in the cloud-tumbler determine how water molecules get added to its structure, and so whether the snowflake eventually finds itself as a tree, a star, a plate or a column.

Each flake emerges from its formative cloud with a unique orientation to the ground; each falls from a different point in the sky. Falling, each meets different atmospheric conditions. Each shape rides the air currents uniquely, traversing the sky for a unique time and across a unique distance. Each crystal has an individual presence that makes it more or less attractive to other flakes that may glom onto it, making a bigger, clumsier flake. The snowflake may fall through another, warmer, cloud, where more water vapor condenses and freezes onto the crystal like rime, weighting it down and making it fall faster.

Falling, each snowflake follows a unique path reflecting its origin, the way it presents itself to the world, and the context that it lives through. So some flakes float; some swirl. Some plummet; some dance. Some slide up and down the scales, as light and fleet as a Lester Young sax solo.

Landing, the snowflake may fall softly into a drift, to be pawed, pushed, and packed into a snow tunnel by a squirrel searching for a faintly-remembered acorn. Or it may softly fall onto a horizontal tree branch, ready to shine with its fellows as a line of light glinting in the next day's bright clearing sun. It may be wafted by a microbreeze into the current of a stream to decorate the surface, sequin-like, before yielding its autonomy to the surrounding flow. Or it may be knocked sideways by the nearby passage of a larger flake into the path of a sleepy skunk just out for a breath of fresh air, where it settles onto the white stripe − unless the skunk is walking the tiniest bit faster so it settles onto the black stripe.

No two beginnings are the same; no two paths align; no two endings are alike.

And so I wait, open-mouthed, as the snowflake descends. Falling softly, softly falling.

Winter Paths

From my window I look down on the narrow backyard, a scroll of blank snow that over the course of the day records and reveals purposeful movement. Tracks appear where juncos, sparrows and finches on seed-gathering expeditions have traced paths on the back porch up to the coir welcome mat, around the flower pot, on the railing across the short gulf from the pole feeder. Through the yard they go, up and over the oak tree stump, along the fence, under the azalea and around the garden statues. Each is a record of intention, the shortest distance between multiple points: a complex algorithm that incorporates relative risk from watchful cats and potential reward from the steady supply of the feeder or the chance that new windblown seeds are hidden under the mat... the likelihood of meeting a competitor, the safety in numbers of the flock vs. the potential bonanza of the lone grubstake. Not just tracks, but graphs of probability and possibility, the calculus of a life lived.

The forms of trees stripped bare of leaves are tracks as well, journeys in search of light. Time has etched the path of yearning into static shape, a trail of decisions made, neighbors accommodated, opportunities taken. A complex calculation is at work within the tree, too. A tree is a single organism but also a collection of chemicals that interact with each other, a communications network. Information about the availability of sunlight and nutrients is conveyed throughout the tree by hormones that either stimulate, or inhibit, growth: every new branch will use resources that the tree could otherwise use to grow taller, and vice versa, but new branches, with all their additional leaves, also represent potential sources of new energy. Shoots start growing from buds only when the result of the multivariate branching equation says "now."

Winter traces the paths of water into solidity. Drop by drop down the tree branch, the rock face, and the rain gutter, dripping water slows to a halt; little by little the icicle forms, suspending water's inevitable passage to ground. …High above in the sky, vapor finds a drifting particle of dust; water molecules spin and turn, aligning themselves into orderly crystals: the unique shape of each snowflake represents the path that each molecule took and the atmospheric conditions of its journey…. Exhaled breath is a cloud of droplets, the hidden constituent of air and the body, now made visible as life lends energy to that which gives it being; the beat of time exposed as a series of clouds.

Winter is when time slows and stops, when the eternal present finds itself surprised by evidence that it is now past, when the promise of the future hangs in a drop of frozen water at the end of a tree branch: a seed, a flutter of wings.

A Fête For the Fetid

Which season's signature flower is the most precious? Hepatica, the first of our spring ephemerals, annually recreates the first flower ever, presaging the explosion of life. Poet Thomas Moore immortalized the last rose of summer (before he killed her, and "kindly" scattered the leaves). Autumn is the season of the witch, when the spindly yellow-fingered blossoms of our native witch hazel beckon, "Here, my pretty."

Winter – cold, gray, bleak, unending winter – begs for something to look forward to, a crumb of joy to relieve the deprivation of the cold, gray, bleak, unending succession of days. And indeed – eureka ! – winter provides it.

Winter

I started hunting in January. I bushwhacked through the woods, down to the floodplain by a stream, and began searching. I looked, not in the flowing water itself, but in the sloping banks and sediments where the water table is high. During winter this swampy ground is usually frozen, so it's easier to walk on. Yet one must walk very carefully, measuring each step, to avoid crushing young plants – or just stand still, surveying by turning only from the neck up. There's nobody else around; wetlands walking is a blessedly solitary activity: no one glances suspiciously while I'm swiveling owl-fashion or hunched over like Igor, lurching from this likely spot to that one, halting every so often to mutter "I know you're here somewhere..."

I knew they were there, because I'd seen them there before. Skunk cabbages emerge year after year in the same place. They're among the longest-lived plants we know; like trees, they endure for decades, even centuries. Penn's Woods could be full of skunk cabbages that witnessed the Walking Purchase. Their development is the inverse of trees, though, with the growing portion concealed below the surface. The stem is a swollen underground rhizome with a Medusa's mane of roots. The roots are contractile: they pull the stem down into the ground, so as it ages more and more of its mass is hidden.

As I searched, I glimpsed a few miter-like conical projections of rolled-up buds peeking above ground. Here was confirmation that this was still a fruitful spot, reason to keep looking, to scan again from a different angle...Aha! a full-fledged bloom at the base of a tree. I knelt to honor it. No matter the season, seeing a hoped-for flower for the first time all over again brings a rush of gratitude. Faith rewarded, the cycle completed and begun again.

The skunk cabbage flower shape is like two cupped hands rising vertically from the earth. As with jack-in-the-pulpit, wild calla and other members of the arum family, what appear to be petals are really modified leaves: sheaths of a tent-like spathe surrounding a club-shaped spadix (the "jack" of jack-in-the-pulpit) on which tiny flowers form. The spathe's color is typically a deep burgundy – solid, mottled or striped with white or yellow. Shiny, waxy and smooth, it invites a gentle stroking.

To fully comprehend the essence of skunk cabbage you need to bend way down and catch a whiff of its unique fragrance. The "skunk" of its common name is more aptly applied to the odor of the leaves that appear later in spring; the flower smells more like dung or rotting flesh. That, plus the bloom's resemblance to carrion, ought to be sufficient enticement for the pollinating flies wakened by late winter or early spring thaws. But the skunk cabbage provides an additional incentive: it creates its own warmth, keeping the interior of the tent a comfy 72 degrees no matter the weather outdoors. It's a veritable ski chalet, a winter haven for insects.

In February I discovered a whole new colony in a wetlands that I'd just begun to explore. My first forays were unpromising. I wasn't finding the Goldilocks spot – not too dry and not too wet. Then I noticed the mahogany-colored dried fertile fronds of the sensitive fern, which shares the skunk cabbage's fondness for woodsy wetland margins. Drawn by the fern flags, I followed a streamlet to a wide flat area hummocky with frost heaves. There I spotted one crimson tent, then another, then another – I was surrounded. I let out a whoop. Of course, there was no one to hear me. These wetlands exist only because they're of no use to anyone. Squeezed between the useful ballfield and the useful parking lot, the skunk cabbage persists, thrives and hosts its insect parties.

Skunk cabbage pursues its own individualist ways: flowering in winter, growing underground, smelling putrid, thriving in waste places. The cold, the dark, the dead, the unwanted: skunk cabbage transforms these elements into enduring beauty. No more precious flower exists.

In the Flow

Late winter runs a backstitch through the fabric of the year. Longer, warmer days alternate with freezing nights. One step forward, one smaller step back, advancing inexorably toward spring, pulling a thread moistened by flowing sap.

In early February, I spotted a yellow-bellied sapsucker tapping at trees around my house. It was the time of year when groundhogs are accorded the status of oracles who foretell the impending spring. But in this area, the sight of a sapsucker truly heralds the coming vernal incline of the Earth toward the Sun. A member of a woodpecker species that is rarely seen in southeastern Pennsylvania in winter, this bird must have been migrating north, anticipating the cusp of the seasons. The other members of the woodpecker family normally observed in our region (the downy, the hairy, the red-bellied, and in deep woods, the pileated woodpecker) are year-round residents. All the woodpeckers share a proclivity for drilling into trees. But whereas the other woodpeckers are harbingers of decay, sapsuckers presage rebirth. The others probe dead or dying wood for insects; sapsuckers excavate neat round holes in living trees, searching for the elixir they love: the sap. Their regularly spaced drill pits may extend across the sunny side of a tree like a row of buttons. It's the sunny side of the tree that gets warm during the day, which is crucial. Frozen sap doesn't flow. Until the days are warm enough to thaw the sap that freezes overnight, drilling is futile.

Spring sap is born of the push-and-pull between moon and sun. Icy winter nights are lit by the frozen blue of the Sap Moon; days are warmed by the rejuvenating Sun. In some species of trees, the freeze-thaw cycle simply loosens the sap that is frozen within cell walls, so it begins to flow. In others, such as the sugar maple, the cycle causes carbon dioxide bubbles in the wood to contract, then expand; freezing sap forms a frosty coating around the bubbles, and when warmed bubbles expand they force sap out of wood fiber cells. A wound or hole in the tree that penetrates into the sapwood creates a point of negative pressure that induces the sap to flow out, whereupon it may be collected and boiled down to sugar syrup. Maple trees produce the most concentrated sugar sap, but hickory, birch and butternut trees also can be tapped in spring, as was customary among indigenous peoples of our region. They may have learned this practice from observing the sapsucker at work.

Having left its calling card, my sapsucker moved on, continuing its northward journey. By mid-March, warm days had begun stringing themselves together like embroidery. Tender fingerling leaves of spring beauties, green tinged with matchstick red, poked out of the earth. The male goldfinches were sporting bright yellow courting feathers mixed in with their grayish brown winter duds. Spring seemed on the verge of bursting out. Yet a hickory tree in the yard appeared to be weeping and black circles ringed holes in its bark. Why such melancholy, an inappropriate welcome to this most delightful of seasons?

Examining the tree closely, I could see that however lachrymose the hickory's state might be, these were not the tears I would cry, nor the tired eyes I would cast upon the world. These tears were drops of sap; the dark circles were congregations of tiny ants surrounding sapsucker drill pits. Ants were thronging about the pits, waving their antenna and stamping their feet, as excited as a crush of traders at a commodities exchange. From each hole stretched a line of ants marching up and down the tree trunk; the lines merged into a single parade that disappeared into the ground a dozen feet away. Along the way, each ant that met with one going in the opposite direction stopped to converse – touching and rubbing the antennae of the other.

It was the sugar in the sap that the ants were after – summer sugar. During the growing season, the tree photosynthesizes sugars from sunlight and water; as dormancy approaches and growth slows, it stores the sugar as starch in its wood, bark and roots. When winter begins to turns into spring, starch turns back into sugar, which dissolves in the sap. A bountiful summer yields a sweet spring; like a jar of strawberry preserves, sap is a time capsule for the palate.

Push and pull, back and forth, warm and cold, the year advances haltingly, like a procession of ants stopping and starting, the one going one way greeting the one going the other way. Nature's time is neither all a line nor all a circle, it's a bubble expanding and contracting, taking in and giving back.

I bend to the tree. A blob of amber-colored sap no bigger than the head of a pin is held in tension at the edge of a drill hole, just inside the red-orange inner bark layer.

The ants haven't yet clustered around this hole in great numbers; there is room to reach in with a twig and grab a globule of sap. A bit of wood adheres to the drop, a remnant of the drilling that brought it forth. The sap tastes of tree, of sun, of moon, birds, and ants; of then and now and what is to be. My cup runneth over.

Dance at Dusk

Late winter, at dusk, has a neither-here-nor-there quality. It is not yet spring, but spring's damp warmth is rising in the soft air, even as winter's chill tugs it back down to earth. It is not daylight anymore, nor is it yet night; still - there is more day than there was yesterday, and more to look forward to tomorrow.

This is woodcock time. And there is a woodcock place just like it. An in-between place that is not woods, not meadow, not pond, but the not-here, not-there land of the edge. Ten acres where low-growing shrubs and dense grasses form brushy thickets, where the ground is wet but not underwater, layered with gobs of decaying leaves. This place is not developed, not farmed, not preserved; surrounded by houses and roads and a vestigial farm field, it exists on the margins.

In this in-between-time, at this in-between-place, the woodcock's mating ritual anchors time and place. At twilight, its nasal, buzzy "peent" call floats over the field. It is not a melodic sound, like that of a songbird, but neither is it harsh like a jay's. It catches your ear's attention, rather like an orchestra conductor rapping the baton before a performance. The "peent" (which is also often rendered as "beezp") is repeated several times, then the woodcock rises up from the ground, flying in widening spirals. At dusk it is hard to see, but you can follow the flight by ear: the bird's feathers create a fluttery whistling sound as it flies round and round. The flight typically ends after half a minute; as it descends, the bird calls again with a burst of warbling, squeaky "cheeps" like kisses. Then the dance begins again; performances can go on all night and into the morning.

The male woodcock goes through this elaborate ritual to attract a mate. He shows off his prowess, and starstruck females flock to his doorstep. What he needs, what this place provides, is a stage that gives him space to dance. To hide their nests, the females need cover, which is provided by the brush. Both males and females need a reliable source of food, and here the wet, rich earth yields copious amounts of earthworms, the mainstay of the woodcock diet year-round.

Having observed the woodcocks one year, I now look forward to their arrival. The season begins to have that quality of turning. Cardinals now greet the dawn with a cheery piping song. Skunk cabbage pokes up its purple knees above the mudline. It just feels like the right time to start listening for them.

Knowing that they should be here, now, gives this time and place its own identity. The calendar may say March, and the clock may say 6 p.m, but the time is "woodcock courtship begins"; the map may say we are in Buckingham Township but the place is "where the woodcocks dance."

So when I hear them, my heart lifts. My pleasure in observing this complicated, choreographed ritual is made more poignant by the knowledge of the rightness of it, that this is a unique time and a unique place, a time and place expressing the nature of the woodcock.

If we listen hard enough, every time and place has its own identity. That time early one morning when the buttery sunlight falls on the dewdrops, outlining spiderwebs stretched overnight across the faded heads of goldenrods. That place where at midnight in a clear, moonless winter sky the Pleiades were straight up overhead like a cloud of ice crystals.

I want to catch and grab onto this time and place, to hold onto it so it cannot disappear into memory. But that would be to destroy it. Like the woodcock's dance, its beauty lies in the spiral that you cannot see: in the turning and returning, the coming back to this time and this place, the here and now that will be there and then.

Epilogue

Song of the Woods

The song of the veery begins high in the green mist, in the upper reaches of the forest canopy. It enters my consciousness stealthily and without warning, the first few notes soft and deliberate, as if the bird were drilling a small hole in the top of my head and pouring liquid song into it. The notes spiral round and round gathering speed and spinning sound around until the song falls to earth with the mist. It soaks into the ground, and rises with sap in the trees to the bird high in the branches, and when it gets there the song starts again. It sounds of liquid and solid, of up and down, light and dark, cycle and flow, movement and stillness. The trees and the leaves, the water and the soil and the rocks all resonate through it.

The song stops me in my tracks as soon as I hear it, as if the spiraling notes have spun a rope around me and held me in thrall to the singer. I can't help but look up, to where the song starts, feeling the tall straightness of the trees lead me up just as the guidelines on a flower blossom direct a bee's attention to the nectar at the center. The veery is the sweet spot at the heart of the forest.

Where oh where is the bird that makes such music? It must be up there but I see nothing, nothing but green leaves. The veery's woods are deep, and moist, and thick with foliage. The woods are deep on the ground, too, the kind of forest you can't see through: all the better to provide cover for the veery's nest near the ground, and for its insect-foraging activities down in the dirt and debris, down where its olive-brown drab merges with dust and detritus, disappearing into duff.

A veery's home need not be wilderness, but it must be larger than a neighborhood park – at least a "hundred aker wood." I've heard the veery in Bucks County on the forested ridges in and near Nockamixon State Park; in Mercer County on the slopes of Baldpate Mountain, in the Musconetcong Gorge in Hunterdon County, and in the Wissahickon Gorge in Philadelphia.

In all these places, and more, I've heard the song begin, closed my eyes, lifted my head, and given myself up to be held by it. In all these places, when the song begins, the world as it is at that moment ends. It ends and then begins anew with this sound like the start of being. The song sung by an invisible singer.

And what good would it do, really, to see the bird sing? Pay no attention to the bird behind the leafy curtain. It's the song that matters. Not the credit. Why do we feel compelled to know who made the artwork? who painted the picture, or wrote the poem,   or composed the music?

When we try and hear the bird, not the song, we lose the music.

Recordings of the veery fall flat. The voice sounds tinny, muffled, one-dimensional. Something is missing.

An iridescent pebble shimmers in a sunny stream. But dried and set on a shelf, it's dull. Removed from the place that gave its spirit voice through the light charmed by the constantly shifting, flowing energy of water, it turns mute.

Don't bother digging a lady's slipper orchid from the woods; it won't grow elsewhere. Its roots can't absorb nutrients without the fungi that only live in the soil where that particular orchid grew. The underground filaments are invisible, but the showy flower that depends on them flaunts her bright pink billowy bloom graced with curlicue tendrils. Down below, the fungi toil in secret. She is their song.

The veery's song excised from the woods is sound, but not music. In the woods, it is not the veery that sings. It is not birdsong that resounds. It is the woods that is the composer. The trees and the leaves, the water and the soil and the rocks, and all that lives above and below. It is the forest itself that sings its own song; the veery is its voice.

Notes

The essays collected in "Now" and the Epilogue were originally published in the *Bucks County Herald* and the *Doylestown Patriot* between 2001 and 2011 as the occasional columns "Nature's Way" and "The Nature of Bucks." "Here" was written to accompany them. I've made minor revisions, corrected errors and typos, but not modified the essays to reflect changed circumstances.

The common names of species of birds are often capitalized in the ornithological literature, as are the names of plants in botanical literature, but I have used lower case.

p. 4. Edward Hicks painted more than 60 versions of the *Peaceable Kingdom*, in addition to the one illustrated here, c. 1834. Courtesy National Gallery of Art, Washington, images.nga.gov.

p. 5. Throughout the book I use the spelling "Lenape" to refer to both the Lenape Nation and the language. An alternative spelling, Lena'pe, reveals the proper accent on the second syllable. The Lenape Nation of Pennsylvania now maintain a cultural center in Easton, PA. See lenapenation.org.

p. 52. Since the original publication of "Golden Locks and Red Sox," Yaz's accomplishment was matched, in 2012, by (future Hall-of-Famer?) Miguel Cabrera of the Detroit Tigers.

p. 63. The Paunacussing Preserve provides only limited access to the public. natlands.org/preserves-to-visit/other-nature-preserves

p. 112. Robert Red Hawk Ruth is the Chief of the Lenape Nation of Pennsylvania. See note to p. 5.

p. 167. To hear the recorded song of the veery, go to allaboutbirds.org/guide/Veery/sounds.

Acknowledgements

Many of the essays in *The Wild Here and Now* were first published in the *Bucks County Herald* and the (now-defunct) *Doylestown Patriot*. My heartfelt thanks to Bridget Wingert of the *Herald*, and to David Campbell, formerly of the *Patriot* and now at the *Herald*. My dear late friend Ralph Copleman enabled a number of these pieces to be further disseminated through the *Sustainable Lawrence* website.

Much gratitude to my father, David Charkes, who encouraged me to follow through with this project, my mother, Nancy Charkes, an insightful and generous reader of my work, and Dagmar Gundersen, a great editor and friend.

www.ingramcontent.com/pod-product-compliance
Lightning Source LLC
Chambersburg PA
CBHW050124280326
41933CB00010B/1241